COLUMBUS HISTORY

A Journal of the Columbus Historical Society

Volume 1, No. 2

Fall 2023

ISBN:978-1-7366917-5-5

Columbus Historical Society
717 West Town Street
Columbus, Ohio 43222
(614) 224-0822
info@columbushistory.org

Columbus History
A Journal of the Columbus Historical Society
Bob Hunter, Editor
James Tootle, CHS publications committee chair

CONTENTS

From the Editor

Several years ago, I was at dinner with a large group of my newspaper colleagues. Someone asked about the research process for a book I had written about Chic Harley, an early Ohio State football hero, and my frequent visits to the library became a topic of conversation.

"You know, I'll bet I haven't even been in a library in 30 years," a fellow sportswriter replied. He giggled, as if it were a badge of honor.

As one who had benefited enormously from library resources for decades, I should have called him out for that. I should have explained that  if I had to choose between a professional sports team or a public library in my community, the team would have to start packing. Seriously. Instead, I think I uttered a feeble "Really?"

I'm grateful to have a chance to rectify that mistake now. The Columbus Metropolitan Library is celebrating its 150th birthday this year. A quick glance at the cover of this issue of *Columbus History, A Journal of the Columbus Historical Society*, provides a visual hint at how long the library has been an important part of this community. The two-dozen people in the photo are utilizing the library's reading room around 1900.

Bob Hunter

Columbus could never have become a great city without its library. In the early days, the presence of a public library made a profound statement about a community. It showed that it valued education, science and literature, that it was a place where knowledge was available to all.

The history of the Columbus Metropolitan Library that CML Local History and Genealogy Manager Angela O'Neal and CML Special Collections Supervisor Aaron O'Donovan compiled for this issue chronicles the ways the library has evolved over the years. From a single reading room with newspapers and a small collection of books it grew into the sprawling 22-branch, multi-dimensional place that it is today.

Early library supporters such as John and William Desher and John W. Andrews would be amazed at the incredible library system that Columbus has now and justifiably proud of the surety of their vision. They didn't take the presence of a library for granted, and neither should we.

Bob Hunter is editor of *Columbus History* and has been a member of the Columbus Historical Society Board of Trustees since 2011. He is the author of numerous books, including *The Road to Wapatomica, A modern search for the Old Northwest*, and is a former sports columnist of the *Columbus Dispatch*. He can be reached at bhunter@columbus.rr.com.

Remembering. . . the Deshler Hotel

.   David Deshler bought the lot at the northwest corner of Broad and High Streets in 1817 for the then-exorbitant price of $1,000, 10 times the price of most lots, and the young carpenter built a wooden house and shop on the site that survived until 1878. David's son, William Deshler, built the four-story Deshler Block that year, a brick building which housed the Deshler Bank, storerooms and offices. Then in 1912, William's son, John Deshler, announced plans for a 400-room hotel – 269 with baths -- that would rival the finest in the world at the time. The Deshler Hotel's opening on Aug. 23,

1916, was a gala affair; 102 chefs, waiters and captains were hired in New York and were brought to Columbus in chartered railroad cars and the 525 guests were entertained by opera stars and an international dance team. The hotel was leased to Ohioans and New York hoteliers Lew and Adrian Wallick and advertised for years as "the most beautifully equipped in America." There was no denying its elegance. The lobby floor was decorated by a

Beasley-Deshler Hotel in 1968

mammoth Oriental rug that cost $15,000 in 1927. The Wallicks added 600 rooms in the new AIU building – known today as the Leveque Tower – next door, which was reached via a "Venetian bridge" at the second story level. The hotel was renamed the Deshler-Wallick. New York mayor Jimmy Walker came for the opening and tried to have a ceremonial sip of wine in each of the 600 hotel rooms; legend says he almost did it. President Harry S. Truman spoke here in 1946 at a conference of the Federal Council of Churches of Christ. As former President, he and wife Bess Truman stayed here on July 6-7, 1953, during a three-week road trip from Missouri to the East Coast and back in a 1953 Chrysler. The hotel was sold in 1947 to Chicagoan Julius Epstein, who sold it five years later to the Hilton hotel chain and it was renamed the Deshler-Hilton. In 1964, a company headed by Charles Cole bought and renamed it the Deshler-Cole. Cole eliminated the 600 rooms in the Leveque Tower and remodeled the hotel, but its decline was underway. It was sold one last time to Fred Beasley in 1966 and became the Beasley-Deshler. But it was closed in 1968 and was razed in September, 1969. One Columbus Center, a 25-story office building, stands on the site today.

Main Library building in 1930

COLUMBUS METRO LIBRARY: FREE AND 'OPEN TO ALL' FOR 150 YEARS

BY ANGELA O'NEAL and AARON O'DONOVAN

One hundred fifty years ago, shortly after the cruel crucible of the Civil War, a group of dedicated citizens formed the first free, public library in our capital city. The Public Library and Reading Room opened on March 4, 1873, as a single room inside the original Columbus City Hall. Those modest origins were born out of a simple idea — to provide people access to the resources they need to enrich their minds and transform their lives and their communities.

Columbus has a storied history of supporting libraries. Calls for a public library in Columbus grew with the population of the city. As early as 1821, the *Columbus Gazette* reported that "the apprentices of Columbus" came together to form a library. Other early libraries were subscription-based or supported with proceeds from lecture series. In 1835, the Columbus Reading Room and Institute was established with access to books, newspapers, and periodicals. The business plan was to support the reading room through fee-based lecture courses. By 1839, however, the *Ohio State Journal* announced that the venture had ended because the reading room could not attract enough paying patrons. Other ventures of circulating libraries were the Western Lyceum and the Franklin Lyceum.

One of the most promising efforts was the opening of the Columbus Atheneum in the Franklin County Courthouse in 1853. It was supported by private contributions and proceeds from lecture series. Speakers included Ralph Waldo Emerson and P.T. Barnum. The library for the Columbus Atheneum was more successful than previous libraries because it was supported by the officers, who were able to purchase a large collection of books for the reading room.

By 1856, the library had moved to the Deshler building at the southeast corner of High and Town Streets to accommodate nearly 1500 books. The collection was so large that the library employed a librarian to help patrons find materials. The Atheneum was a successful endeavor for many years, but by 1871 the lecture series had been dormant for a long time and the library was in debt at the time of closure.

With the closure of the Columbus Atheneum came an opportunity to create a truly free public library for all citizens of Columbus. On June 15, 1871, library advocates met in the old City Hall to plan an appeal to City Council for funds for a public library that would be free and open to everyone. The ordinance to establish a library space in City Hall passed and the library opened on March 4, 1873.

John W. Andrews, the first president of the library board of trustees, emphasized that the library would be "open to all" at the

John J. Pugh (center) was hired in 1881 and became chief librarian when Rev. James Grover retired. Blanche Roberts (front row, second from left) became the first woman employee in 1893 and the first female chief librarian/director in 1946.

dedication ceremony. He said, "I congratulate you. . . our City Council, backed by the unanimous voice of the citizens, has established and liberally endowed a free library and reading room, free to the whole population of the city."

At the time, City Hall was located at the current site of the Ohio Theatre. One room was set aside for the library. Rev. James Grover, pastor of St. Paul's Episcopal Church, was named the first librarian and paid a salary of $800 per year. He was the library's only staff member until 1879. When Grover retired, John J. Pugh, who joined the staff in 1881, became chief librarian. Blanche Roberts became the first woman employee in 1893 and the first female chief librarian/director in 1946.

The 1872 ordinance establishing the library also included the appointment of a board of trustees. Four board members were selected by

The Henry C. Noble alcove

City Council, and there were three ex-officio members, which included the mayor, the president of the Council and the president of the Board of Education. The first board included Otto Dresel, Alfred S. Glenn, William B. Hayden, and John W. Andrews, as well as ex-officio trustees Mayor James G. Bull, Board of Education President Fred Fieser, and Luthor Donaldson, president of the City Council.

In 1890, the state legislature passed the "Heffner Ripper Law" that disbanded some city-appointed offices, including the library board. The board was re-established in 1891, although the Board of Education no longer appointed an ex-officio trustee since it had formed a new school library. In 1902, the State of Ohio passed a law on municipal codes that changed how all city library boards in Ohio were established. The mayor would select six trustees, and there was bipartisan agreement that no more than three trustees would be from the same party. Board members also had to live in the city of Columbus.

Contributions from citizens were part of the library's history from its founding. Soon after City Council passed the ordinance to fund the library, a "victory party" was held and raised $49 for books and supplies. At the library's dedication in 1873, Board President John W. Andrews encouraged fellow citizens to give to the library and said their gifts "will bless successive generations of citizens and will have an influence on children and children's children." The Deshler family was the first to make a large contribution to

Groundbreaking for the Main Library occurred on October 12, 1903. It took nearly four years to build.

the library. In memory of their father, John and William Deshler donated $1,200 to support the purchase of books, with the stipulation that the library "shall remain public and free to every resident of Columbus, without distinction of race, sex, color or religion." Early gifts came in the form of "alcoves" where donors would sponsor the purchase of a collection of books. Eighteen alcoves were created: Deshler, Noble, Hubbard, Andrews, Brickell, Kilbourne, Women's Music Club, Medical, Dental, Mattoon, Lyman, Sessions, Battelle, Mooney, Moore, Braun, Stevenson, and Soldiers & Sailors.

Until 1891, the original library included the Columbus City Schools' library. Even after the school library moved out, the library was overcrowded with books and customers. In 1896, the city appropriated funds to expand the space using vacant land to the east of the building. Visits continued to grow to nearly 100,000 with 13,000 cardholders. By 1900, the library was running out of space again.

As more people used the library, it was clear that Columbus needed a new building. The Board tapped chief librarian John Pugh to meet with industrialist Andrew Carnegie to ask for funds to build a stand-alone library. Carnegie typically funded rural or branch libraries. He funded over 100 public libraries and eight academic libraries in Ohio. It was not clear if he would consider funding an urban library. However, when Pugh met with Carnegie in New York, they bonded over their shared experiences as sons of immigrants. Although the meeting went well, several months passed with no word from Carnegie.

On December 31, 1901, Carnegie wrote a letter offering $150,000 to go toward building a new library, with the condition that the library board find a suitable site and the city appropriate at least $20,000 per year for maintenance. City Council quickly passed a resolution for the maintenance fee and the board set out to find a location.

The initial suggestion was to build the library at the corner of State and Third streets, across from the Statehouse, but ultimately land for the library was purchased at State Street and Grant Avenue. The T. Ewing Miller property was purchased for the site of the new Carnegie library. The site was also known as Swayne Mansion and served as the first governor's mansion. The home was built circa 1847 for attorney Noah H. Swayne. He was later appointed a justice of the Supreme Court by Abraham Lincoln.

Albert Ross, who worked with Carnegie on many library projects, was selected as the architect for the new building, Wilbur T. Mills was supervising architect. Although the original plan for the library included a brick façade, the board asked Carnegie to fund another $50,000 for marble to make the building "an ornament to the city."

The Columbus Public Library building was dedicated on April 4, 1907 and regular library service began on April 8. The new library included an auditorium and space for exhibits and cultural displays. It was considered fireproof, since the only wood used was on railings leading up to the second floor and down to the basement. Until 1931, the library was home to the Columbus Gallery of Fine Arts, the predecessor to the Columbus Museum of Art. The gallery hosted exhibits of artists such as Alice Schille and Emerson Burkhart. The Carnegie Gallery continues to be used for art exhibits today.

The new library quickly became a community gathering place. During the 1913 flood that devastated the city, the library registered family members who were separated from loved ones and worked to reunite them. When City Hall burned in 1921, the mayor, city council and other government offices moved to the library's basement until the new City Hall building opened in 1928. During World War II, the library served as Columbus' official civilian information center. It was also home to the Franklin County Historical Society (now known as COSI) from 1948 to 1956.

Shortly after the new library building opened in 1907, it became clear that Columbus' many neighborhoods needed branch libraries. Horse-and-buggy traffic along Grant Avenue led to congestion, and hitching posts near the library were often at capacity. Also, Columbus residents wanted library locations closer to their homes. However, Andrew Carnegie was no longer funding libraries and City Council did not have funds for branches.

The board of trustees decided to create library "deposit" locations in fire stations, settlement houses and schools. The Godman Guild became the first deposit location in 1910. It and other locations had between 100 and 500 books for visitors to read. Other locations included Bellows Avenue Recreation Center, the Crittenden Home, the B'nai B'rith Social Center, the Hague Avenue School, the Juvenile Detention Home, and the South Side Settlement House.

After World War I, there were repeated calls for branch libraries. Fred J. Heer, president of the library board, appealed to the Federation of Women's Clubs for help. On January 17, 1928, the women marched to City Hall to demand funding for branches. Two weeks later, City Council appropriated $40,000 to build four branches: Clintonville, Linden, Parsons, and Hilltop. Public response was enormously positive. Within 10 years, the combined annual circulation numbers of the branches exceeded those of Main Library.

A house built by attorney Noah H. Swayne in 1848 was torn down to build the library in 1903. It was home to Ohio governors, including Rutherford B. Hayes.

A new department was created as a result called Extension Services. Rose G. Beresford was tapped to lead it in 1928, and she served in that position until 1942. Under her leadership, the Milo Branch opened in 1930 at the start of the Great Depression. The economic downturn took a toll on libraries: staff took a 50 percent pay cut and purchases of new books and materials virtually ceased between 1930 and 1939. As a result, State Senator Robert A. Taft drafted a bill that allowed library boards to request funds from their county commissioners if libraries offered services county-wide. The law passed in 1933 and in July, 1934, Columbus Public Library became a county-wide library.

To support library services around the county, new facilities called "county stations" were established. They were typically a room in a school and were often staffed by teachers. Canal Winchester was the first county library station in 1937. It was followed by Briggsdale, Dublin, Fornof, Gahanna, Galloway, Harrisburg, Hilliard, Lockbourne, New Albany, and Reynoldsburg.

As the library expanded county-wide, the board organization changed as well. In 1976, Columbus City Council voted to create the County Library District. The Ohio Revised Code's library board requirements for county library districts went into effect, providing the structure that exists today: the Franklin County Board of Commissioners selects four trustees, and the Franklin County Court of Common Pleas selects three. Trustees have a term of seven years. Annie Norton Battelle, the first woman trustee, joined the board on February 1, 1920, and at least one woman has served on the board ever since. In 1934, three women served as trustees together for the first time: Elizabeth Norman, Cora Brickell, and Lora Kirk. The first time the board included four women trustees was 2022: Katie Chatas, Sandy Doyle-Ahern, Catherine Strauss, and Carla Williams-Scott.

Equipping young readers has been an important goal of the library since the library's earliest days and Summer Reading is one of the oldest recurring programs at the library. One of the most gratifying accomplishments for Head Librarian/Director John Pugh was the creation of the Children's Department in 1907. With a dedicated space in the new Carnegie building, the Children's Department created displays and programs for children of all ages to enjoy, like "Story Hour," which was first held in 1909.

In 1937, children's librarians Blanche C. Roberts and Lillian Skeele developed a reading contest to keep children engaged during the summer months when they were not attending school. The first official "summer reading contest" took place at Columbus Public Library's Main Library, May 15 - July 15, 1937. The 165 participants ranged from third to eighth grades. The program had a baseball theme, with participants' names entered on a large scoreboard so they could see their place in the standings. Prizes for the top readers were books donated by library staff.

After a successful first year, the library decided to make Summer Reading Club (also known as Vacation Reading Club), an annual event. The second contest was extended to children from third to twelfth grades and

The Milo Branch at 768 Leona Avenue was dedicated on January 18, 1930 as the system's fifth branch. It was replaced by a bookmobile stop in 1950. Most of the book collections was donated to the Franklin County Children's Home.

was open to kids at Main Library, Hilltop, and Linden branches. In 1942, the number of books participants needed to read to "graduate" was reduced from 15 books to 12, and the library extended the program to all branches and county station libraries.

The 1950s saw a surge of participants in Summer Reading Club: themes changed and staff promoted programs in locations. In 1951, it was extended to customers who accessed the library through the bookmobile, which made 29 stops around the county. In 1953, the library began to bring in guests to promote Summer Reading Club. Among them was "Aunt Fran" Norris, a children's television show host on WBNS-TV. Norris was a popular personality and precursor to Luci's Toyshop. In 1955, the zoo theme attracted over 9,000 sign-ups from 10 branches and 83 bookmobile stops. The prize for reading 10 books was a free one-day pass to the Columbus Zoo.

Summer Reading Club continued to grow in the 1960s and 1970s under the leadership of Phyllis Thompson. One of the library's first Black librarians, Thompson became head of the Children's Department in 1968. Expanded programs included more Storytimes, adventure and nature movies on Saturdays at Main Library and the Bookworm Club for students who had completed fourth, fifth, and sixth grades.

In 1976, free coupons for fast food were given to children who read 12 books. The library aired its first television commercial for 1979's Summer Reading Club, featuring a superheroes theme. Superheroes Word Woman and Super Reader fought villain Dr. Dolt, who was stealing books from library shelves. The library initially ordered 10,000 custom t-shirt transfers proclaiming "I'm a Super Reader" to give participants after they read 12 books. By the end of the program, the library had awarded 75,000 transfers.

Summer Reading Club entered the 1980s with a roar with the theme "Bring a Dinosaur Up to Date." Other themes of the decade included "Join the Space Reading Crew" and "Reading is Cool." In 1988, the entire summer was dedicated to a Maurice Sendak celebration. In 1981, just over 8,000 children registered for the program; by 1989 that number had increased to almost 18,000.

In 2018, Summer Reading Club's name changed to Summer Reading Challenge, featuring the Reading League, a team of pro-literacy caped crusaders. Superheroes such as Captain Read and Page Turner encouraged everyone to make reading a habit. All ages participated by reading, completing activities, and attending programs. The library's locations came alive with music, filled up with laughter and celebrated special guests, including artists, magicians, goats, and even hedgehogs! It proved to be the perfect blend of fun activities and reading to prevent summer learning loss. During 2020 and 2021, Summer Reading Challenge changed to navigate the obstacles faced by the COVID-19 pandemic. In-person activities moved

By 1960, five bookmobiles like this one checked out over a half million books in one year. By 1969, bookmobiles served 118 locations in the county.

online and prizes were mailed to homes. In 2022, the library resumed its in-person Summer Reading Challenge and more than 40,000 kids, teens, and adults registered.

Columbus experienced enormous growth after World War II ended in 1945. Enrollment at The Ohio State University tripled and the population of Franklin County grew to over 500,000. In 1951, when the library celebrated the 50th anniversary of Andrew Carnegie's gift, it was clear that more space was needed at the Main Library, especially for cataloging and outreach services. Council member Henry Koontz, who remembered borrowing books from Main Library soon after it opened in 1907, led the effort to raise funds for a building addition. Although construction was delayed a year due to restrictions on purchasing steel because of the Korean War, the new library service building opened in 1953. A second addition was built between 1959 and 1961.

Bookmobile service began in November 1950 to reach parts of the county that were not served by a library branch or county station library. In its first year, over 75,000 books were borrowed from the bookmobile. By 1958, there were four bookmobiles that together made up one-quarter of all library circulation that year. In 1995, two bookmobiles were redesigned to become "Metro Mouse Mobiles" and visit area preschools to promote early literacy skills. The last two large bookmobiles were retired in 2014. One small bookmobile is still in use for library sponsored and community events. Home delivery service began in 1972 and continues as a mail service for customers who are unable to visit in person. Lobby Stop service to senior residential sites began in 1995. Many of the original sites are still on the roster. Delivery of classroom collections of books to 23 area schools began in 2014 and became part of Outreach Services in 2016.

With the additional space at Main Library came new services and technological advancements. Long before computers, the library helped citizens gain access to new technology. The Microfilm Reading Room opened in 1948 with one reader and several cabinets of microfilm. Record and film collections began in the 1950s, and the library purchased its first Xerox copier in 1966.

Reference services in the 1970s and 1980s saw many advancements, from new electronic resources to innovative access tools. The library's first public computer was installed in 1977. Staff in the Business & Technology, Magazines & Newspapers, and Fine Arts divisions responded to thousands of customer questions each year. The expanded Columbus and Ohio Room was dedicated in 1975 to answer local history and genealogy questions.

The library's focus on youth continued in the second half of the 20th century. Storytimes, teen events, and programs for preschoolers expanded. At Main Library, the Center for Discovery opened in November 1978 to "give very young children a chance at development before they start school." It featured a treehouse, story pit, and puppet theater. Journalist and author Wil Haygood later wrote, "On Saturdays my grandmother would give me money to catch the bus downtown to go to the Main Library on Grant Avenue. There were always school projects that took me to the big library to do research! I'd dive into the history and art sections, scouring for books. History fascinated me. So did maps."

As the library grew, its name changed to keep up with the times. The 1873 ordinance that created the library simply called it the "Public Library and Reading Room." In 1903, the stand-alone library was named Columbus Public Library. In 1976, the Board changed the name to Public Library of Columbus and Franklin County to reflect the inclusion of county libraries. In 1989, the Board changed the name to Columbus Metropolitan Library, as it remains today.

Funded by the passage of a 2.2 mill levy in 1986, another expansion of Main Library began in 1987. This resulted in the general footprint of Main Library that exists today. There were two phases because buildings behind the library had to be torn down and the parking garage built. The new library expanded from 87,000 square feet to 255,400 square feet of much needed space. The expanded Main Library officially opened on April 13, 1991, with a "Celebration of the Family" that included a breakfast Storytime and alphabet-shaped cakes. Events continued for more than a week, including programs with artists Aminah Robinson and Todd Slaughter, local history

WLWC-TV (now WCMH-TV) donated a film collection to the library in 1970. Head librarian Edward Daniels (left) and Martin Luther King branch librarian Verdi Fitz accepted the donation.

classes, and a wellness fair. The library was officially dedicated on Tuesday, April 30, 1991 in a ceremony that included First Lady Barbara Bush, Ohio Governor George Voinovich, and Columbus Mayor Dana Rinehart.

In the 1990s, many new services incorporated digital databases and internet connectivity. The first online library services began at Main Library, including the creation of an online catalog. The library launched its first website in March 1998 so library customers could access services at home. Supporting authors remained a central part of library services as well. The library has hosted many notable authors over the years, including Marc Brown, Jason Reynolds, and Diana Gabaldon. Others include Bill Bryson, Ashley Bryan, Bob Greene, and Jeff Kinney. The library has also sponsored author talks at other venues in Columbus, including events with Toni Morrison and Rick Steves.

In April 2007, Main Library celebrated the 100th anniversary of its April 1907 grand opening. To mark the occasion, the library held two events. On April 21, the Columbus Metropolitan Library Foundation hosted the Party of the Century black-tie gala on the library lawn. Guests enjoyed dancing and dinner by Chef Hartmut Handke. Then on April 28, the Friends of the Library held a Community Open House with cake and ice cream for everyone. Those attending enjoyed activities for all ages. The library was also recognized with a historical marker. Several thousand people visited the library during this centennial celebration.

Library services continued to expand to meet community needs in the 2000s. In 2004, the first Homework Help Center opened at the new Linden Branch; by 2012 all locations had Homework Help Centers. The library began offering eBooks on OverDrive in 2005; nearly 600 eBooks grew to a collection of 10,000 eBooks, audio and video files by 2010. In May 2013, the library joined the Central Library Consortium, giving customers access to more than a million more resources, including books, audiobooks, DVDs, and CDs. In 2018, the library gained access to SearchOhio, a consortium of public libraries and OhioLINK, a consortium of Ohio's college and university libraries. Borrowing also became easier during this time. Automatic renewals began for checked out items in 2014. On January 1, 2017, the library stopped charging fines for overdue books and other materials because overdue fines often prevented people, especially kids, from using the library.

On February 24, 2015, Main Library's newest renovation kicked off with a wall breaking event. The renovation connected the library to Topiary Park, reimagined the Children's area, created more meeting and study rooms, and featured a new Reading Room to host author talks and events. The removal of the exterior marble from the front and back of the library revealed spectacular views of downtown and Topiary Park. The project was part of CML's 2020 Vision Plan, developed in 2009 to address and prioritize the needs of its aging locations and the evolving community demands upon them. Phase I renovated or rebuilt 10 of CML's 23 locations, including Main Library. Phase II included renovating or rebuilding four additional branches.

The 2016 renovation of Main Library made it a popular location for big events such as Cartoon Crossroads Columbus and the Ohioana Book Festival. The Carnegie Author Series hosted dozens of authors and filled the Reading Room with customers who love to read. In July 2023, the Columbus Metropolitan Library hosted its first Big Book Festival, which drew over 25,000 visitors to Main Library.

In 2023, the Columbus Metropolitan Library celebrates its sesquicentennial, 150 years of service to Central Ohio. The library held Birthday Bash events on March 4 to kick off the yearlong celebration and created a Sesquicentennial Passport program for customers to celebrate throughout the year. Community partners such as the Columbus Museum of Art, Columbus Symphony, and CAPA are celebrating with the library with free community days and events. A special Sesquicentennial Author Series features Julia Quinn, Silvia Moreno-Garcia, Saeed Jones, and others. In addition, the library installed a temporary public art vending machine, called the Egg Prize at Columbus Commons.

As Ohio's capital city, Columbus continues to experience incredible

On April 30, 1991, First Lady Barbara Bush, Ohio Governor George Voinovich. and Columbus Mayor Dana Rinehart spoke at the dedication of the remodeled, expanded Main Library.

growth. Planning studies estimate that the Columbus region will gain one million new residents by the year 2050. The current U.S. Census Bureau results report that Columbus' population grew more than 15 percent from 2010 to 2020 making Columbus one of the fastest growing cities in the Midwest, and one of only 14 cities nationwide to gain at least 100,000 residents during that time frame. Intel's recent announcement that it planned to build a "mega-site" on 1,000 acres in Licking County also heralds a new age of growth for Central Ohio and its workforce.

What does this mean for Columbus Metropolitan Library's vision of a thriving community where wisdom prevails? It means the library keeps growing and keeps innovating. It has an enduring history of evolving to meet customer needs as the world around it changes. Community activism resulted in the library's expansion from a single reading room to central Ohio's largest library system at 23 locations. Community support continues to help the library provide access to books, resources, technology -- and knowledge -- so each location can be a space that meets the promise of the words etched above Main Library's front doors – "Open to All." Library work is steeped in the tradition of service; the future of that service is shaped by the wants and needs of the people who walk through the doors of every library, every day.

Cartoonist and author Jeff Smith wrote, "the Library of the Future is here today. Thanks to the digital media revolution, libraries have transformed into architecturally interesting and inviting spaces. Peaceful. Calm gathering places for the curious who seek out knowledge, while providing access to all the information that now resides in the clouds. Naturally, the library of the future still has books and most importantly, librarians. The future is good."

Angela O'Neal is the manager of Local History & Genealogy at the Columbus Metropolitan Library. She has a master of library and information science degree from Kent State University and is a graduate of the History Leadership Institute and Leadership Columbus. She has also served as president of the Society of Ohio Archivists, Chair of the American Library Association's Local History Committee and is a former member of the Ohio Humanities and Columbus Historical Society boards of trustees.

Aaron O'Donovan is the special collections manager in the Local History & Genealogy division at the Columbus Metropolitan Library. Aaron has a bachelor's degree in sociology from The Ohio State University and a master's of library and information science from Kent State University. Aaron specializes in Columbus history and digitization. He has presented at conferences including those for the Community Webs program at the Internet Archive, The Best Practices Exchange, the Ohio Library Council, and the Society of Ohio Archivists. He also has appeared numerous times on the PBS affiliate WOSU Columbus Neighborhoods series as a digitization and local history expert.

CHIEF TARHE CAMPED, HUNTED, AND TRADED IN AREA

By BOB HUNTER

Wyandot chief Tarhe, the Crane, can justifiably be called one of history's great Native American leaders. But he is remembered in Central Ohio – when he is remembered at all – for the events of one afternoon, June 21, 1813. That was the day he assumed leadership of fifty tribal chiefs and warriors who came to Franklinton to meet with Major-General William Henry Harrison during the War of 1812. But the characterization of Tarhe as something of a one-hit wonder is both understandable and untrue.

Tribal leaders came to Franklinton at the invitation of Harrison, commander of the United States' Northwest armies against Britain. Harrison, whose headquarters were in a house on what is today's West Broad Street in Franklinton, gave an emotional speech beneath a giant elm tree on town founder Lucas Sullivant's property. Harrison asked Ohio tribes to refuse to fight on the British side. Shawnee brothers Tecumseh and Tenkswatawa (The Prophet) had already created an Indian confederacy that was fighting on the side of the British. So getting the Wyandot, Seneca, Delaware and Shawnee tribal leaders who assembled in Franklinton to pledge to remain out of the war would provide a significant boost to the Americans.

Harrison was surrounded by his officers, all dressed in full military regalia. A detachment of soldiers stood behind them, all at attention. The Indians sat opposite them, many of them smoking pipes and paying little attention to the future president, who started his speech in calm and measured tones, urging the natives to either move deeper into the nation's interior or join the American cause against the British. Nervous settlers watched and listened. Many remembered what it had been like to have Indians surprise a sleeping family in their cabin in the middle of the night, ambush farmers in their fields or kidnap their children. They didn't want to return to those harrowing days again.

A tortured silence followed the close of Harrison's remarks. Finally,

Tarhe, the Crane

Tarhe, the venerable, 71-year-old chief of the Wyandots, rose slowly, said a few words and then gave his hand to the general in a token of friendship. The tense settlers recognized this as agreement with Harrison's plea for either peace or help. As the other Indians moved forward to shake hands with the general, cheers of relief filled the air. Women wept, children laughed and a scene of joyous pandemonium followed. For those living in an isolated area in the middle of the Ohio frontier, it was a spectacle they would never forget.

While this historic scene played out on Sullivant's lawn in Franklinton, likely in what is today a parking lot east of Souder Avenue and south of West Broad Street, the infant village of Columbus was being carved out of the forest on the east bank of the Scioto River a mile away. The Ohio General Assembly had chosen a site for the new state capital only 16 months before and it had only been one year since the first lots were sold. Franklinton residents Lyne Starling, John Kerr, James Johnston and Alexander McLaughlin had offered the site to legislators and agreed to spend up to $50,000 to build a statehouse and other buildings. Franklinton, which had

also been proposed as the state capital site and had been eliminated because of the threat of flooding, was annexed to Columbus in 1870.

It's incredible to think of the different course local history might have taken if Tarhe and his allies had decided to abandon the pledges they had made at the Treaty of Greenville in 1795 and side with the British now. It's one reason why Tarhe's name is probably familiar to long-time Columbus residents who have at least a cursory interest in local history.

Harrison elm, as it appeared when F.H. Howe photographed it in 1892. Hawkins Hospital (later Mount Carmel) is in the background.

But Tarhe had a much deeper relationship with this area than that fateful day in Franklinton and his personal history is such that it deserves considerably more notice than he receives from most modern Ohioans.

Tarhe was born in 1742 of humble beginnings near the French settlement of Detroit. He belonged to the Porcupine clan of Wyandots, one of 12 ancient clans of a tribe descended from the Petuns, or "Tobacco Nation." The tribe had a connection to the Huron-Wendat through its lineage from the Attignawantan, the founding tribe of the Huron.

Tarhe, nicknamed "The Crane" by the French because of his angular 6-foot-4 frame, became a warrior at an early age, fighting new settlement in the Northwest Territory. Not much is known of his early life, although some historians speculate that he fought with his tribe in British General Edward Braddock's defeat in the Battle of the Monongahela in 1755 when Tarhe was only 13 years old. The Wyandots were prominent in that fight, and the Ottawas were led by Pontiac there. Tarhe supported and fought on the side of Pontiac eight years later at Detroit, so it makes for intriguing speculation that Pontiac may have taken notice of him at that early age.

Tarhe led fifty Wyandots as part of Pontiac's tribal confederacy in the siege of Fort Detroit in 1763 and likely participated in the nearby Battle of Bloody Run. He fought alongside Shawnee chief Cornstalk in Lord Dunmore's War at the Battle of Point Pleasant (West Virginia) in 1774, a fierce battle in which Tecumseh's father Pucksinwah was killed.

Upon the death of Half-King in 1788, Tarhe became the titular head of the Wyandots, a position known as the grand sachem. Although he was considered an excellent warrior, his election to this position seems to have been more about his character and his leadership qualities than his fighting prowess. He is believed to have been the first member of the Porcupine Clan to achieve that lofty position in the tribe. Grand sachems had always come from the Deer, Bear and Turtle clans.

As such, Tarhe was among Indians leaders including Little Turtle, Blue Jacket and Buckongahelas who led over 1,000 warriors in a rout of Arthur St. Clair's forces on November 4, 1791 on the Wabash River at a spot that eventually became Fort Recovery, Ohio. Of 920 troops, 632 U.S. soldiers were killed in that battle and 264 were wounded – an incredible 97 percent casualty rate -- and 200 camp followers (people who offered support, supplies and other services) died as well.

St. Clair's defeat had followed General Joshua Harmar's embarrassing losses at and near Kekionga (Fort Wayne) the year before (battles in which Tarhe seems likely to have participated). These events set into motion the advancement of Anthony Wayne to the leadership of the American army and the fateful Battle of Fallen Timbers in 1794. Tarhe suffered what has been described as a serious arm injury in that battle (at the site of modern Maumee, Ohio) but was the lone Wyandot chief to survive of the ten who participated.

At a tribal council prior to that momentous battle, Tarhe is said to have spoken in favor of peace. It is the first time we catch a glimpse of the peacemaker who recognized that the tribes' hopes of ultimately driving the white men out of the Old Northwest were unrealistic. Following the battle, he successfully lobbied other tribal leaders to make a preliminary agreement of peace with General Wayne and suspend hostilities until a general treaty could be made. When Wayne called the losing tribes together to sign the Treaty of Greenville in 1795, Tarhe was the first to sign. Harrison, whom Tarhe would come to know so well later, was there at both the treaty signing and at Fallen Timbers as Wayne's aide-de-camp.

In the summer of 2023, Billy Friend, current chief of the Wyandot nation, told a Franklinton Historical Society audience in Columbus: "When the Native Americans gathered in Greenville to sign the treaty, Chief Tarhe

Tarhe's mark on the Treaty of Greenville is directly below signature of Anthony Wayne.

was the first to sign and he was the very first to get up to speak. If you have a chance to Google his speech that day at the signing of the Treaty of Greenville, it was where he said 'We are going to bury the hatchet.' He said he would never take up arms again against the U.S. That was significant because of the peace treaty that happened here [in Franklinton in 1813] with William Henry Harrison. Harrison knew the influence that Tarhe had. He

24

had a lot of influence with the Native American tribes and he was very well-respected."

Harrison always spoke glowingly of him. In his report made to the Secretary of War, March 22, 1814, the future president said: "The Wyandots of Sandusky have adhered to us throughout the war. Their chief, the Crane, is a venerable, intelligent and upright man." At another time, while speaking highly of several important chiefs with whom he had been in contact, he described Tarhe as "the noblest of them all."

Tarhe's influence had deep, sprawling roots in the region that became the state of Ohio. Around 1757, Tarhe married Ronyouquaines La Durante, believed to have been the daughter of Chevalier La Durante, a French Canadian who lived on Mackinac Island. Ronyouquaines had been captured by the Wyandots and adopted into their tribe. Their daughter, Myeerah, was born the year of their marriage. Myeerah later married Isaac Zane, who was also captured by Wyandots at the age of eight in 1762 from the Zane family home in Mooresville, Virginia (West Virginia today) and was also adopted into the Wyandot tribe. He lived with the tribe for seventeen years and married Myeerah in Wheeling, Virginia, in 1771. At the time of their marriage, Tarhe's camp was at the site of modern Zanesfield, Ohio, in Logan County near Bellefontaine. The chief reputedly gave his camp to the newlyweds and moved to another Wyandot camp, Soloman's Town, in the north central part of the county. Isaac Zane laid out the town that became Zanesfield.

Tarhe's first wife died in 1803 and he later married Katy (Sally) Sage. Sally had been abducted from the family cabin on Elk Creek in Grayson County, Virginia, when she was five years old. They had one child together, a developmentally disabled son who died at the age of twenty-five.

Like most tribes, the Wyandots were frequently on the move. Sometime during this period before Fallen Timbers and the Treaty of Greenville, Chief Crane, as some called him, lived in a Wyandot camp on the Hocking River at the site of present Lancaster, Ohio. That camp was called Tarhe Town. By the time of the Battle of Fallen Timbers and the treaty signing, Tarhe had apparently moved his base camp to Lower Sandusky, modern site of Fremont, Ohio. He appears to have lived there sporadically until around 1810, when he moved to the Upper Sandusky area (Upper Sandusky, Ohio), the site of his base camp until his death in 1815.

When Tarhe was traveling from the Sandusky region to the village of Chillicothe or to Franklinton, he often camped for long periods at a grove on the west bank of the Scioto River in today's Columbus. The grove had a spring nearby. The property is in an area of a handful of houses on Carriage Lane (an eastern extension of Hilliard-Cemetery Road), about a mile north of Fishinger Road.

The site of Tarhe's camp might have faded from history were it not for the Sells family. Ludwick Sells and wife his Catherine (Deardorff) Sells came to Franklinton from Huntingdon County in central Pennsylvania about 1802 with other members of the family. Franklinton was a stopping off point for many prospective settlers in those days, a place to live while they scouted the region for available property.

Most of the Sells family eventually settled in Washington Township in the vicinity of today's Dublin, 14 miles north. Son John Sells platted the original village on his property. In 1810, John and brothers Benjamin, Peter and William tried to stop the execution of Wyandot chief Leatherlips by six Wyandot warriors from Michigan, including chief Round Head, allegedly for practicing witchcraft. Historians believe that Leatherlips' refusal to join Tecumseh's confederacy and fight against the Americans is the real reason for his death sentence. Leatherlips' camp was not far from the Sells brothers' cabins.

William Henry Harrison

In 1831, historian B.B. Thatcher wrote the book *Indian Biography: Or, An Historical Account of Those Individuals who Have Been Distinguished Among the North American Natives as Orators, Warriors, Statesmen, and Other Remarkable Characters* in which he accused Tarhe of ordering the death of Leatherlips. In 1838, he reiterated this theory in an article titled "Doomed Warrior" in the first issue of *The Hesperian, or, Western Monthly Magazine*, which was published in Columbus. When Harrison read this, he wrote a long letter to the editor of the publication, in which he emphatically disputed Hatcher's characterization of the events. In reference to Tarhe, he wrote:

"I knew Tarhe well. My acquaintances with him commenced at the Treaty of Greenville in 1795. His tribe was not under my superintendence in the year 1810. But they had been from the year 1800 until the year 1807 or 8, and were again subjected to my direction soon after the commencement of the late war with Great Britain. All the business I transacted with [the tribe] was done through Tarhe.

"I have often said I never knew a better man, and am confident he would not have been concerned in such transaction as is ascribed to him. . .
"

Harrison then offered five detailed reasons why Tarhe wouldn't have done it, including the fact that he had always been an "opponent" of Tecumseh and Round Head, and concluded with:

"The party sent to put the old chief to death, no doubt, came immediately from Tippecanoe; and if it was commanded by a Wyandot, the probability is that it was Round Head, who was a Captain of the band of

26

Wyandots who resided with the Prophet."

Although the Sells' oldest brother Samuel wasn't part of the Leatherlips story, he has an indirect role in the Tarhe story as it relates to Columbus. Samuel lived in Franklinton for several years before eventually moving in his brothers' direction. While he lived in Franklinton, Samuel might well have met Tarhe because early accounts say that Tarhe was a friend of Lucas Sullivant and a frequent visitor to Franklinton. Neither is surprising because many Native Americans came there to trade.

Samuel's son Abram was born in 1806 in his parents' log house in Franklinton; he has been called the first white child born in Franklin County. The cabin stood a block and a half southeast of West Broad Street and Sandusky Street (now the 315 freeway). That would likely place the cabin in the vicinity of today's Grubb and Shepherd streets, or about one thousand feet east of the tree that the 1813 peace conference would turn into a local landmark called the "Harrison elm."

According to the *History of Franklin and Pickaway Counties, Ohio*, published by Williams Brothers in 1880, Samuel moved about a mile west of Dublin on Indian Run in 1809. But a *Columbus Dispatch* story about Abram in 1903 indicated that "he made the log house of his parents (in Franklinton) his home until he was married at the age of twenty to Miss Louisa Brown. Abram and Louisa then settled into a home of their own on the Hilliards pike, (today's Hilliard-Cemetery Road) about a mile east of Hilliards (Hilliard)."

If true, that means seven-year-old Abram and his parents were living in Franklinton in 1813 when Harrison hosted his peace conference and it increases the likelihood that any or all of the family attended. At least one of Samuel's brothers (Peter), seems also to have been living in Franklinton during this period, so if Tarhe hadn't already made an impression on the Sells family, he may have done so that day.

Abram and Louisa moved to their place east of Hilliard in Norwich Township shortly after they exchanged vows. Several years later – and this is where Tarhe re-enters the story – Abram bought a farm near the intersection of Hilliard and Dublin pikes (today's Dublin Road), which included the old Tarhe camp site.

Although Tarhe had long been dead at that point, he doubtless lived in the memories of several members of the Sells' family. Abram Sells called the grove of trees near the river and the spring Wyandot Grove because of the Tarhe connection, and in 1879, a large gathering occurred there that may have been a forerunner of the Wyandot Club.

In a story in the September 1, 1879, *Columbus Evening Dispatch* headed "Pioneer Picnic," the newspaper reported that this was more than a day to consume a little lunch next the river:

"Wyandot Grove is the name given to a well-watered and shaded

The Scioto River at Wyandot Grove in 1897. The Wyandot Club clubhouse was located on the nearby shore.

spot on the farm of Abram Sells, six miles from Columbus, up the Scioto River. It is the identical spot upon which stood the wigwam of Chief Crane, who ruled a detachment of Wyandot Indians. Besides the two springs, one of which is said to possess medicinal qualities, there is a mile stretch of deep water in the river and two islands.

"Rev. James Spicer was president of the pioneer picnic held at this spot, Saturday. On motion of Peter Sells it was decided to designate it the Scioto Valley Pioneer Association, auxiliary to the Franklin County Pioneer Association. The following officers were chosen: Daniel Thomas, President; Fletcher Sells, Vice-President; Abram Sells, Secretary; W.A. Crim, Assistant Secretary. It was then decided to hold the next annual meeting of the association at the same place, on the second Sunday in August, 1880.

"Speeches were made by General James A. Wilcox, Messrs. Abram Sells, F.C. Sessions, Peter Sells, James Lawson, Rev. James Spicer and others. Mr. Sessions, in the course of his speech, said his grandfather was one of the party of persons who threw the tea overboard in Boston harbor. Mr. Abram Sells spoke of his knowledge of the Indians. Mr. Peter Sells was present in the first common school opened in the county, and was a member of the first Sunday school opened in Columbus. James Lawson was an early stage driver and punished a large quantity of liquor, but he said he was a different man now. Old Aunt Agnes Brown, colored, supposed to be about 110 years of age and who came from near Charlestown, Va., in 1825, was the recipient of much attention. Mr. Fletcher Sells prepared a poem for the occasion, but arrived too late to read it to the whole audience."

The club met again in 1880, and after that, no more mention of it is made in the papers. But the Wyandot Club was started in 1881 with seventeen members and held its annual meeting and dinner in the same location until it disbanded in 1923. Its seventh reunion on September 18, 1887, attracted notice in the *Dispatch*, and was the first time that public notice was given that the group was concerned about the ignominious ending that came to beloved Wyandot chief Leatherlips. In 1889, the group purchased a one-acre plot of ground six miles north where Leatherlips had been executed and buried in 1810, and erected a granite monument to his memory. It's still there on the east side of Riverside Drive, just to the south of Stratford Drive, a quarter of a mile south of the Columbus Zoo. (In 1990, the Dublin Arts Council erected a 12-foot high, stacked-stone depiction of Leatherlips' face on the west side of Riverside Drive in Scioto Park.)

Alfred E. Lee's 1892 book *History of Columbus, Capital of Ohio*, took notice of that 1887 meeting, Leatherlips and Tarhe's camp on the Scioto:

"In Columbus (there) is a social organization called the 'Wyandot Club.' Its officers are, President, William Taylor; Vice-Pres. A. McNinch; Secretary, E. L. Taylor; Treasurer, G. W. Willard. Among their intentions is to perpetuate the memory of Leatherlips, by the erection of a monument on the place of his execution and burial, which is about fourteen miles north of Columbus near the Delaware county line.

"Steps were taken for this purpose at their annual reunion, September 18, 1887. This took place in a noble forest named 'Wyandot Grove' on the west bank of the Scioto about eight miles northwest of the city, with about 150 invited guests, where under a spreading tent they sat

The Wyandot Club erected this monument in 1889 near the site where Leatherlips was executed and buried. It still stands in a small park east of Riverside Drive, a quarter of a mile south of the Columbus Zoo.

down to a sumptuous repast gathered from the farm, garden, river, and tropics, amid which the florist made a gorgeous display.

"This feast had been preceded by a speech by Col. Samuel Thompson, in which he gave a sketch of the noble Wyandot tribe, the most humane of all the Indian tribes, and largely opposed to the torture of prisoners. He paid a tribute to one of their great chiefs, Tarhe, or Chief Crane, so wise in council, and so renowned in war, and who had interposed in vain to save the ill-fated Col. Crawford from the stake. 'I learned,' said he,

This Leatherlips sculpture by Boston artist Ralph Helmick was placed in Dublin's Scioto Park in 1990.

'from our venerable friend, the late Abraham [Abram] Sells, former proprietor of this beautiful grove, rightly named by him Wyandot Grove, near your crystal spring once stood the cabin of this noted chief. It was here that the Wyandots halted to rest and refresh themselves when on their way to the white settlements at Chillicothe and subsequently at Franklinton, this county.'

"The Colonel then told the story of Leatherlips, who was executed 'for political reasons,' substantially as already given. He was followed by Capt. E. L. Taylor, who spoke in a very interesting manner, after which a committee was appointed to take measures for the erection of the monument."

The club purchased 40-acre Wyandot Grove from Joseph Sells (Abram's son) in 1894 for $3500. In 1894, club members built a stone and shingle clubhouse here with a dock attached to the back so members could come and go by boat on the Scioto River. Once a year, the club hosted a huge party with 100 or more guests and Tarhe was one of the primary topics of conversation. In 1899, the city purchased 11 acres of the property with the intent of building a 58-foot dam, but plans were scaled down to one of 38 feet. The new height brought the river just to the clubhouse doorstep, so there is some thought the wealthy club members had exerted their influence.

The club had a limit of seventeen members, so the only chance anyone had to be admitted to the group came when one of the members left or died. The limitation ultimately made it difficult for the group to maintain membership. It eventually disbanded in 1924 and one of the club members, Emil G. Buchsieb, bought the property. He died in 1956. The clubhouse burned August 12, 1974.

Several houses occupy the property today, which might distress Tarhe but probably wouldn't surprise him. He recognized the ramifications of the increasing influx of white settlers before many of his contemporaries did and realized the tribes had little chance of stopping the tide.

He was near the end of his life when he gave Harrison his hand in peace in June, 1813, and he stuck to his word and led his Wyandot warriors in Harrison's campaign in Canada that ended with the death of Tecumseh on October 5, 1813, in the Battle of the Thames. Tarhe was 71 years old and living in a cabin surrounded by woods in Crane Town, four miles northeast of Upper Sandusky at the time.

The settlement was on the east bank of Crane Run, which emptied into the Sandusky River. Tarhe lived in a log cabin, fourteen by eighteen feet, surrounded by a dense forest. The old gauntlet ground lay a short distance south of the cabin and west from the village site was a clearing of about ten acres known as the Indian field, also surrounded by a dense forest. Tarhe died in that cabin in 1815.

Tarhe's service drew what was called the largest crowd ever for the funeral of an Indian chief. In the book *Recollections of Sixty Years*, Indian agent John Johnston described the funeral and the general council of tribes that followed it:

"I was invited to attend a general council of all the tribes of Ohio, the Delawares of Indiana, and the Senecas of New York, at Upper Sandusky. I found on arriving at that place a very large attendance. Among the chiefs was the noted leader and orator Red Jacket, from Buffalo. The first business done was the speaker of the nation delivering an oration on the character of the deceased chief. Then followed what might be called a monody or ceremony of mourning and lamentation. Thus, seats were arranged from end to end of the large council house, about six feet apart. The head men and the aged took their seats facing each other, stooping down their heads almost touching. In this position they remained several hours. Deep, heavy and long continued groans were commenced at one end of the row of the mourners and were passed around until all had responded and these repeated at intervals of a few minutes. The Indians were all washed and had no paint or decorations of any kind upon their person, their countenance and general deportment denoting the deepest mourning. I had never witnessed anything of the kind and was told this ceremony was not performed but upon the decease of some great man."

Jeremiah Armstrong, who lived in Franklinton and Columbus from its earliest settlement until his death in 1862, had a more personal relationship with Tarhe.

Armstrong was captured by the Wyandots near Blennerhassett Island in the Ohio River in modern West Virginia as a boy and wrote a narrative of his experience for William T. Martin's *History of Franklin County Ohio*. He had just turned nine in April 1794 when he and his older brother and sister were captured and carried into Ohio by a party of twenty

Wyandots. His mother and other members of the family, except his father, were murdered. In the Wyandots' retreat they passed the points of Lancaster, Columbus and Upper Sandusky en route to Lower Sandusky, where Tarhe was chief. Armstrong wrote:

"On arriving at Lower Sandusky, before entering the town, they halted and formed a procession for Cox (a fellow prisoner), my sister, my brother and myself to run the gauntlet. They pointed to the house of their chief, Old Crane, about a hundred yards distant, signifying that we should run into it. We did so, and were received very kindly by the old chief; he was a very mild man, beloved by all."

Jeremiah was adopted by Tarhe's tribe:

"After our adoption, the family to which I belonged came back to Columbus and camped near where the Ohio Penitentiary now stands (near the Scioto River on West Spring Street). There we raised corn in what is now Sullivant's Prairie. My home was with them back and forth from there to Lower Sandusky."

Armstrong was back in Lower Sandusky in August when the Indians were defeated at Fallen Timbers, and Tarhe was brought back to their Sandusky Bay camp, "wounded in the arm." A year later, when the Treaty of Greenville was signed, hostages were supposed to be released. But when his brother, Bill, found him the Wyandots' camp in Lower Sandusky, "he found me so much of an Indian that I would much rather have seen him tomahawked than to go with him. Old Crane would not consent to give me up. He said that according to the treaty they were not obliged to release any that were willing to stay. They agreed to go to Brownstown (Michigan) and examine the treaty."

His brother went to Detroit and appealed to the general there, who gave him an officer and twelve men to secure his release, and they met Jeremiah and the Indians at Brownstown. His brother, John, had also been brought there and both were taken by William against their wills. Later after William had refreshed their memories with stories of their capture and their family members' deaths, they changed their attitudes and willingly accompanied their brother William to Detroit, Pittsburgh, a neighbor's house near their old home, Chillicothe and finally to Franklinton, where brothers Robert and William were both living.

Jeremiah turned twenty-eight in 1813 and bought a lot on South High Street in Columbus between Rich and Town streets and opened a respectable hotel and tavern there under the sign of Christopher Columbus. It was later called the Red Lion Hotel and became a popular lodging spot for William Henry Harrison, Henry Clay, [U.S. Senator] Thomas Ewing and several Ohio governors. Jeremiah and his brother Robert were both elected

Tarhe is believed to have been buried near the location of this monument, erected in his memory in 1915. He was living in a cabin here in Cranetown when he died.

to the first Columbus City Council in 1816. Until his death, Jeremiah is said to have always retained a great reverence and affection for Chief Crane.

The exact location of Tarhe's burial is unknown. Jonathan Pointer, a Black man who had been a captive among the Wyandots and who fought alongside Tarhe in the Canadian campaign under General Harrison in 1813, claimed that he assisted in the burial of Tarhe on the John Smith farm, about a half mile southeast from his cabin home. He said that logs were dragged over the grave to keep the wild animals from disinterring the body.

In 1915, the Tarhe Tribe, No. 145, I.O.R.M. (Improved Order of Red Men) fraternal organization erected a granite monument to Tarhe on the west side of one-lane Township Highway 37 in the vicinity of Cranetown and the cabin where he died. It identifies him as a "Distinguished Wyandot chief AND Loyal American" and says that "He died here in Cranetown in 1818," a date recent research has shown to be incorrect.

The Sandusky River lies on the other side of the road and Cranetown has long since been consumed by corn fields. In the latter part of summer, a north-facing visitor sees the corn rows veer to the left to give a few feet of space to the monument of a chief whose determination to stay true to his word helped the Americans win the War of 1812

Bob Hunter is editor of *Columbus History* and has been a member of the Columbus Historical Society Board of Trustees since 2011. He is the author of numerous books, including *A Historical Guidebook to Old Columbus,* and is a former sports columnist of the *Columbus Dispatch.* He can be reached at bhunter@columbus.rr.com.

IT'S MADISON TIME!

Columbus was birthplace of a line dance
that swept across America in the 50s and 60s

By **DOUG TRACY**

Columbus claims a number of firsts. Those include the first junior high school (Indianola Junior High in 1909), the first kindergarten (1838 by German settlers), the first filling station (Standard Oil of Ohio at Young and Oak streets in 1912), the first banana split (Foeller's Drug Store at 567 North High Street), the first Miss America (Mary Catherine Campbell in 1922), the first Wendy's restaurant (1969) and the first gorilla born in captivity ("Colo" in 1956 at the Columbus Zoo).

Now you can add another one: According to William "Bubbles" Holloway, Columbus was the birthplace of the Madison, a dance that he created and introduced in late 1957 at his Long View Athletic (LVA) Club on East Long Street in the city's Bronzeville neighborhood. Holloway's story was chronicled in an article by Lucius E. Lee in the June 18, 1960, edition of the *Ohio Sentinel* titled "Madison Dance Started in Columbus." But it was quickly challenged by some folks in Baltimore, who claimed that teenagers in their city spawned the dance. Could it be that both Columbus and Baltimore have a case?

Those who were teenagers in the late '50s or early '60s may remember the Madison as a line dance that was the biggest dance craze of that era, not just in the United States but around the world. Others may have seen John Waters' 1988 movie *Hairspray* or the television series *American*

Madison Dance Craze Started Here In Columbus Town

THE MADISON DANCE craze, which is sweeping the U. S. and Europe, was started in Co-lumbus, says William (Bubbles) Holloway, pictured at left as he calls steps during the early days of the fascinating routine at the LVA Club on E. Long st. Pictured is the first known official Madison team, according to Holloway. From left: Carla Singer, Irvin Jones, Mary Autry, Wallace Jones, Patricia Hodge, Billy Gilchrist, Deanna Early and Eugene Green.—Pierce Photo.

Dreams (2002 to 2005) and witnessed kids on the dance floor in their madras shirts, skinny ties and bouffant hairdos, stepping in sync to "The Madison Time."

Line dances have a long history of popularity, dating back to the Bunny Hop in 1952. Later came the Electric Slide, Macarena, Wobble and Boot Scootin' Boogie. The Madison's closest predecessor may have been the Stroll, another line dance that swept the nation in 1957.

The Madison is a basic back-and-forth shuffle done in a line to a 4/4 beat, with a variety of call-outs for various steps, such as the Double Cross, Rifleman, Cleveland Box, Wilt Chamberlain Hook, Big "M", "T" Time, Daddy Grace, Jackie Gleason and the Birdland. The Madison craze spawned dance teams across the nation and intense competitions from neighborhood to neighborhood and from city to city, much like the Twist in the '50s and '60s, disco in the '70s and break-dancing in the '80s. To this day, the Madison is still taught at many dance studios and it's not unusual to see it performed at reunions, weddings and parties.

When kids across the country were dancing the Madison and coming up with new steps, record companies saw gold to be mined, sparking a flurry of Madison records released by both local and national artists intent on cashing in on the lucrative market. Two hit nationally: the Ray Bryant Combo's "Madison Time – Part 1" b/w (backed/with) "The Madison Time – Part 2" (Columbia catalog no. 41628) and Al Brown and His Tunetoppers' "The Madison" b/w "Mo' Madison" (Amy 804). Even Bill Doggett, whose No. 1 hit "Honky Tonk" sold four million copies in 1956, had "The Madison" b/w "Ocean Liner" (King 5204), but Doggett's version saw only modest chart action.

Al Brown's release on April 4, 1960, took off first, quickly skyrocketing up the charts to eventually peak at No. 23 on *Billboard* and No. 5 on the *Cashbox* R&B charts. Ray Bryant's version was rush-released one week later on April 11, 1960, but climbed only to No. 30 on *Billboard*.

Al Brown was a local Baltimore musician who had formed a jazz group known as the Tunetoppers in the late '50's. The Madison dance was already alive and thriving when Al Brown became aware of it and saw an opportunity to record a song to fit the steps. Brown had seen Baltimore teenagers dancing the Madison outside record shops and soda fountains and came up with a matching song. The recording, on the small Amy label released two weeks before the Ray Bryant version, immediately took off and was a surprise national hit.

Ray Bryant was a major label jazz artist who was the house pianist at the Blue Note in Philadelphia in the early '50's, where he backed many notable jazz greats including Miles Davis, Lester Young and Charlie Parker. He later formed a trio and had some minor commercial success with "Cubano Chant" and "Little Susie." He also issued a stream of well-received LP's but nothing that matched the later chart success of his "The Madison Time."

When "The Madison Time" was recorded by Bryant in 1960, his combo included Columbus's own Harry "Sweets" Edison, a top-shelf jazz trumpeter and graduate of East High School. Edison was at one time a member of Count Basie's orchestra and a session musician who appeared on countless recordings by major artists, including Frank Sinatra, Billie Holiday, Nat King Cole, Bing Crosby and Ella Fitzgerald. The Ray Bryant Madison record also featured calls by Eddie Morrison, who was a DJ in Al Brown's hometown of Baltimore.

Both the Ray Bryant and Al Brown records were strong national sellers, but the presence of multiple versions of the Madison simultaneously on the charts meant that neither would enjoy the number one chart position that might have otherwise occurred for one of them. These two records would prove to be the only top 40 hits for Bryant and Brown, despite their long careers and their many subsequent recordings in the jazz genre.

Ray Bryant's original version of "The Madison Time" saw new life in 1988 as a key part of the soundtrack for the movie *Hairspray*, starring Ricki Lake, Sonny Bono, Jerry Stiller and Divine. In addition to inclusion on the

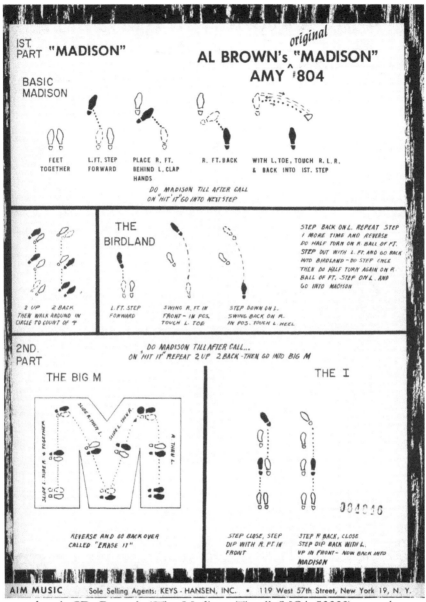

soundtrack CD, Bryant's "The Madison Time" (MCA-53322) was also re-released as a 45-rpm single by MCA that included a picture sleeve showing Ricki Lake and the cast doing the Madison, along with an insert that diagrammed the dance steps.

In 2002, "The Madison Time" appeared yet again in the long-running Broadway production of *Hairspray*, starring Divine and Harvey Fierstein, a production that earned eight Tony Awards. Five years later, in

37

2007, the film version of *Hairspray* was released, starring John Travolta, Michelle Pfeiffer, Christopher Walken, Queen Latifah and Zac Efron.

But were it not for the creative mind of William "Bubbles" Holloway, none of this would have happened. Holloway was a dynamic entrepreneur, club owner and promoter, a well-known figure in the thriving Bronzeville area along Mt. Vernon Avenue and East Long Street in Columbus when his Madison dance took off in late 1957 and early 1958. He always claimed that the Madison was unquestionably his creation, despite claims to the contrary by those in Baltimore. The dates are on his side.

As Holloway related the story to an *Ohio Sentinel* reporter in June of 1960, he was standing in front of the Birdland jazz club in New York City in 1957 with Count Basie's drummer, Sonny Payne, and producer Larry Steele, when he asked Steele how to get to Madison Avenue. Steele's response was

THE ORIGINAL ✱ THE DANCE VERSION
MADISON TIME
RAY BRYANT COMBO   Calls by EDDIE MORRISON

THE
BASIC
MADISON
STEP

It's the swingingest—the zaniest—it's the most sensational new dance in the country

It's "Madison Time." COLUMBIA ♦ 4-41628

"Take it to the left, young man, take it to the left," a phrase that stuck with Holloway. Back in Columbus, with that phrase still resonating in his head, Holloway got together with a group of young LVA Club dancers and, borrowing a couple of steps from the latest popular dance, the Birdland, they came up with a new dance Holloway called the Madison, a rarity among dances in that it starts out on the left foot.

When the Madison began to catch on in the Columbus area, Holloway organized a team of dancers (Carla Singer, Irvin Jones, Mary Autry, Wallace Jones, Patricia Hodge, Billy Gilchrist, Deanna Early and Eugene Green) from his LVA Club and soon had them on the road demonstrating the Madison steps in clubs throughout Ohio. Dancer Wallace Jones was so enamored with the dance that he named his first child, David Madison Jones, after the dance.

The dance troupe's first official appearance was in mid-August of 1959 at Bub's Grill in Cleveland, long after the Madison had already taken hold in the Columbus area. Holloway described the Cleveland appearance as "a sensational hit with the people and from all indications Cleveland will soon be hit with a fantastic Madison craze, the likes of which engulfed Columbus earlier this year." The "Hooks and Slices" column in the August 4, 1960, edition of the *Ohio Sentinel* confirmed that the Madison dance was actually not new – "Columbus dancers have carried the 'CRAZE' to other cities for the past two years."

The *Ohio Sentinel* wrote that the LVA Club's Madison dancers also traveled to Atlantic City, "and showed the audience and cast of that fabulous production of Larry Steele, Smart Affairs, at Club Harlem how to do the dance. They first danced it for the cast and, just that quick, everyone in the audience was doing the Madison." And when Count Basie visited the LVA Club in Columbus in August of 1959 and saw the dance being performed, he immediately imbedded the Madison in his performances when he toured London and other European cities.

Holloway's Madison dance continued to spread throughout the Columbus area, with Madison contests popping up in venues in early 1959. On March 29, 1959, the Merry Makers Club featured a city championship Madison dance contest as part of their annual Easter Dance. Less than two months later, on May 10, 1959, the Cavaliers Club's annual Mother's Day Dance and Revue at Valley Dale sponsored another Madison dance contest, an event that reportedly drew the largest crowd ever seen at that iconic location. Both mid-1959 contest dates are strong evidence corroborating Holloway's claim that the Madison dance was thriving in Columbus, long before the Madison dance records appeared in Baltimore, well over a year later.

It was not until mid-1960 that the Madison erupted in Baltimore when the records of the same name hit local record stores. Bryant's 45-rpm record sold over 200,000 units within the first two weeks of its release. As Holloway had done in Columbus a year earlier, Columbia Records hired two dancers from Baltimore's Buddy Deane show, Joan Darby and Joe Cash, to tour the East Coast demonstrating the Madison steps. The company also created a black-and-white promotional film "Madison Time" featuring the two dancers, a rare film that can still be viewed on YouTube.

At a time when rock and roll was taking over, Bryant's jazz-oriented take on the Madison made it palatable to a much broader audience. The Cincinnati Enquirer's review of the tune was mostly positive, "The purely musical portions reveal a conservative piano by Bryant, some greasy, cloudy, but lyrical and affecting brass solo work in trombone, sax and trumpet, and some engaging fast music from the same quarter." In Baltimore, however, a Sun newspaper reviewer was less kind, "If the Madison words and music are tame compared to original jazz, they are paragons of taste compared to the recent plague called rock and roll. The Brown and Morrison records are free of the hysterical treble and overemphasized pounding of rock and roll and

FROM THE MOTION PICTURE SOUNDTRACK

HAIRSPRAY

THE RAY BRYANT COMBO

The Madison Time

represent a significant popular trend away from it. If the Madison movement helps bury rock and roll, the nation may indeed thank every Baltimorean connected with the dance."

Regardless of the evidence, the origins of the Madison dance continued to be contentious. Despite Holloway's credible story about naming the dance and the indisputable timeline, other sources still claimed that the Madison was named after a bar in Cleveland, a ballroom in Detroit or a street in Baltimore. A *Time* magazine article in April 1960 focused on the story of the dance fad in Baltimore, with no mention of Holloway or of Columbus, an oversight that was repeated when the July 1960 edition of *Ebony* magazine again ignored the Columbus creation. Holloway was infuriated by the snub, prompting Eddie Jay Colston in his *Ohio Sentinel* column of April 16, 1960, to write, "BUBBLES HOLLOWAY has been screaming that 'We wuz robbed' with claims that the Madison was originated here – in his LVA Club."

A year later, Holloway was still fighting for proper recognition, as he pointed out in his December 14, 1961, *Ohio Sentinel* column "The Night Beat", ". . . and to think I tried so hard to permanently implant the Madison

THE NEW **WCOL** DIAL 1230

HITS OF THE WEEK
Columbus' Only Authentic Survey

WEEK OF APRIL 25, 1960

This Week			Last Week
1.	CATHY'S CLOWN ★	Everly Brothers—Warner Brothers	23
2.	BURNING BRIDGES ★	Jack Scott—Top Rank	7
3.	FANNIE MAE	Buster Brown—Fire	25
4.	GREEN FIELDS	The Four Brothers—Columbia	3
5.	THE TIES THAT BIND ★	Brook Benton—Mercury	6
6.	STUCK ON YOU	Elvis Presley—RCA Victor	2
7.	NIGHT	Jackie Wilson—Brunswick	1
8.	HE'LL HAVE TO STAY	Jeanne Black—Capitol	15
9.	LET THE LITTLE GIRL DANCE	Billy Bland—Old Town	4
10.	SIXTEEN REASONS	Connie Stevens—Warner Bros.	5
11.	THE MADISON	Al Brown—Amy	19
12.	CHERRY PIE	Skip & Flip—Brent	26
13.	DON'T THROW AWAY ALL THOSE TEARDROPS	Frankie Avalon—Chancellor	9
14.	WHAT AM I LIVING FOR	Conway Twitty—MGM	18
15.	WHITE SILVER SANDS	The Bill Black Combo—Hi	13
16.	STAIRWAY TO HEAVEN ★	Neil Sedaka—RCA Victor	10
17.	MR. LUCKY	Henry Mancini—RCA Victor	16
18.	NOBODY LOVES ME LIKE YOU ★	The Flamingos—End	11
19.	YOUNG EMOTIONS	Ricky Nelson—Imperial	38
20.	LOVE YOU SO	Ron Holden—Donna	29
21.	TALL OAK TREE	Dorsey Burnett—Era	14
22.	CRADLE OF LOVE ★	Johnny Preston—Mercury	8
23.	THE WAY OF A CLOWN	Teddy Randazzo—ABC Paramount	28
24.	MONEY	Barrett Strong—Anna	12
25.	COMIN' DOWN WITH LOVE ★	Mel Gadson—Big Top	—
26.	THE LEGEND OF THE STEEPLE	Porter Wagner—RCA Victor	32
27.	STEP BY STEP	The Crests—Coed	17
28.	GOOD TIMIN'	Jimmy Jones—Cub	39
29.	MUSIC FOR A PASTEL MOOD	The Wayouts—Top & Bottom	31
30.	NATIONAL CITY	Joiner Ark., Band—Liberty	40
31.	IT COULD HAPPEN TO YOU	Dinah Washington—Mercury	20
32.	FOOTSTEPS ★	Steve Lawrence—ABC Paramount	21
33.	I LOVE THE WAY YOU LOVE	Mary Johnson—United Artists	22
34.	EXCLUSIVELY YOURS	Carl Dobkins, Jr.—Decca	—
35.	ROCKIN' RED WING	Sammy Masters—Lode	—
36.	SWEET NOTHINGS	Brenda Lee—Decca	27
37.	GOT A GIRL	The Four Preps—Capitol	—
38.	I WANNA GO HOME	Jackie deShannon—Edison	24
39.	HOLD ME TENDERLY	Bobby Bland—Duke	—
40.	THATS YOU	Nat Cole—Capitol	—

★ Former WCOL Pick Hit

PICK HIT OF THE WEEK:
MISSION BELL—Donnie Brooks—Era

See Reverse Side for New WCOL Hit Albums of the Week

This survey is compiled each week by Radio Station WCOL, Columbus, Ohio, from reports of all record sales gathered from all leading retail record outlets in the Columbus area. This survey is a true, accurate and unbiased account.

HEAR
RICH PETERS
MIDNIGHT TO 6:00 A.M.

on the floor boards of the world. Lest you forget that I named the dance and popularized it here in the Cap City five years ago. You doubting Thomases can check the *Ohio Sentinel*, the *London Examiner*, or even the *New York Times* for proof."

In the end, the dates do not lie. The dance certainly did become a national "craze" in mid-1960 with the release of Madison records by Baltimoreans Ray Bryant, Al Brown and others, but it is clear that the Madison was well established in Columbus at least a year or maybe two years earlier, the difference being that there was no Madison-titled record to accompany the dance at the time in Columbus. The Madison, designed to work with almost any song with a mid-tempo 4/4 beat, was already alive in Columbus by 1957 or early 1958, even if there was not yet a record of the same name on the radio. The Baltimore Madison records certainly elevated the Madison to a national craze, but it was undoubtedly Columbus where it broke out.

It's time to give Bubbles Holloway and his LVA Club dancers credit. The Madison really did start in Columbus. It's admittedly an obscure bit of Columbus history - maybe not quite as important as the birth of the banana split (which is also contested, by the way) - but one whose claim is corroborated by its timeline. Maybe you can even win a bet at the next wedding reception with this little piece of Columbus trivia.

Doug Tracy is a member of the Board of Trustees of the Columbus Historical Society, the New Albany Plain Township Historical Society and the Toledo Police Museum. His first book, *Wide Open*, is due to be released by the University of Toledo Press in the fall of 2023. He can be reached at dtracy806@gmail.com.

THE WISDOM OF CHARLIE HOOD: 'ALWAYS GIVE GOOD MEASURE!'

City's first Black grocer grew small chain of stores, gave son Earl training to become a successful musician

By **DAVID MEYERS**

Author's Note: Renowned band leader Charles Earl Hood (1896-1991) was 92 when I conducted a three-hour interview with him at his East Side home, not far from Valley Dale Ballroom. But he could have passed for a man 15 or 20 years younger. Remarkably spry for his age, he demonstrated his agility by bending over at the waist and placing the palms of both hands flat on the floor. And his mind was just as agile as his body. Although I was there to learn about Earl's career as a musician, he also regaled me with his memories of growing up in Columbus and especially his father's experiences as the city's first African American grocer. In writing the following account, I also drew upon an earlier interview conducted by my friend and occasional co-author Arnett Howard when Earl was 84.

As Columbus entered the 20th century, it had, according to Earl Hood, three "first class" grocery stores: G.F. Wheeler's Grocery, The McDonald-Steube Company, and Frederick W. Freeman Cash Grocer. Wheeler's was located at 18 North High just above Broad Street, McDonald & Steube's at 98 South High near State Street, and Freeman's at 178 South High Street. The last was nestled between F.W. Bishop's hardware store and Thompson's motion picture house. Within a few years, it would be catty-corner across the street from the brand-new F. & R. Lazarus Department Store.

Eager to make his mark in the world, Charles I. "Charlie" Hood (1867-1912) -- Earl's father -- talked Fred Freeman into hiring him. Charlie started his career in the grocery business at the bottom, literally, sitting in the cellar breaking "spuds" (i.e., sprouts) off potatoes. But Freeman rewarded the hard-working youth by giving him increasingly greater responsibility, eventually promoting him to "solicitor" (or salesman).

In those days, the grocers would send out solicitors in horse-and-buggies to take orders from customers. Charlie got to know the most prominent families in Columbus and also picked up tips from them on how to operate a successful business. It was "Old Man" Lazarus, Earl recalled, who told him, "Charlie, the customer is always right." Simon Lazarus, the store's founder, passed away in 1877, when Charlie was about 10. His two sons, Fred and Ralph, and their mother, Amelia, then took charge and grew the business into one of the greatest of all "Grand Emporiums," or classic department stores.

Charlie would come to regard the Lazarus family as both his customers and his friends. And he particularly valued their business advice. But learning the grocery trade wasn't the only thing he had on his mind: On May 23, 1893, Charles I. Hood and Maud L. Jenkins (1870-1954) were married by Reverend James Preston Poindexter at the Second Baptist Church in Columbus. Poindexter was a former slave and abolitionist who was the first person of color to serve on city council and the board of education during a period of remarkable racial civility in Columbus. Unfortunately, little information has come to light regarding the Jenkins family.

Several years later, Charlie had acquired enough experience and self-confidence to open his own store, The Model Grocery, at 330 East Long Street, in partnership with Merrill L. Cartwright. While it was not in the same league with Freeman's store, Charlie prospered at the location which had previously served as a tailor shop and a storeroom. He was guided by the principle that if he gave honest measure, the customers would come back. And they did.

In 1905, the opportunity arose for Charlie to buy out his partner. Not only did he take full ownership of The Model Grocery on April Fool's Day, but Freemen's as well, rechristening it C.I. Hood's Grocery. He now had a first-class operation in the center of a vibrant city. Although he was black, Charlie had white employees and dealt almost exclusively with a white clientele. Earl said his father experienced few racial incidents, but new customers were sometimes taken aback to discover that the owner of the store was a black man. Meanwhile, Freeman, his former boss, left the grocery business entirely to become a stock broker.

Over the next few years, Charlie bought a half dozen stores, operating as many as three at a time. He owned one at 38 West Town Street, while another was half a day away in Grove City. The latter had been purchased from a German fellow who stayed on as manager. Charlie's three delivery wagons crisscrossed the city from Franklin Park to Camp Chase, and Arcadia to the railroad viaduct on South High. But on February 7, 1910, the

Grocery ad from April 3, 1905 Columbus Dispatch

roof of West & Stevenson's livery stable collapsed due to a heavy snowfall and Charlie lost all three wagons.

Charlie undoubtedly had hopes that his son would follow in his footsteps. Every day after school, Earl rode to work at the store on a bicycle his father purchased from a mail carrier for $7. Having bought bulk goods from Andrus, Scofield & Company, Charlie put the boy to work filling 5-pound bags of sugar from 50-pound sacks, breaking down large bunches of bananas into smaller ones, and candling every egg in the crates of 30 dozen to ensure they were good.

Growing up in this atmosphere had a profound impact on Earl. "All of my associates were white," he said. "To be frank, I didn't know I was colored." He felt that the acceptance he experienced as a black child in a predominantly white community was due to the fact "there was no competitive base," so he was not perceived as a threat. However, that would soon change when a heavy influx of African American recruits from the Deep South were shipped into Fort Hayes due to the approaching World War. This would precipitate a cultural clash, not only between whites and blacks, but between Northern and Southern blacks, that would shape race relations in Columbus leading into the Civil Rights Era.

Earl was proud of his father's accomplishments in the grocery business. He pointed out that his father's store was the first in the area to have a meat slicer. His father also stocked many goods imported from Mexico, which was unusual at the time. However, as Earl told Arnett Howard, "There was a panic in 1908 that wiped out lots of businesses and Dad took sick right after that with malaria and typhoid fever." This was prior to the creation of a central bank so the U.S. economy had to be bailed out by J.P. Morgan, John D. Rockefeller, and other wealthy financiers.

In January, 1909, a mysterious fire broke out in Charlie's grocery, resulting in $2,000 worth of damage to his stock. Six months later, his store in Grove City also caught fire. And in 1910, he was assigned a court appointed receiver, suggesting that he was experiencing serious financial difficulties. The action was initiated by William M. Fisher & Sons, a local produce wholesaler. Fisher was the maternal grandfather of Columbus author James Thurber. In all likelihood, Charlie had fallen behind in making payment for his produce orders.

While Earl acknowledged that he acquired his business acumen from his father, any thoughts he may have had of continuing in the grocery trade were cut short by his father's death from pulmonary tuberculosis on May 12, 1912. A few months earlier, John Henry Hood (1830-1912), Charlie's own father and Earl's grandfather, had passed away as well. Charlie left behind his wife and two sons. It would be a difficult year for the family. However, Earl hung onto a few sepia-toned photographs of the store and the belief that you should always give honest measure in everything you do.

After he left Sammy Stewart's Ten Knights of Syncopation, Earl Hood formed Earl Hood's Oriental Knights. Earl Hood is the standing the back with his violin.

Following Charlie's interment in Green Lawn Cemetery, his widow, Maud (1870-1954), sold the stores. The Model Grocery would reopen as Bee Motion Picture Theater the following year. Meanwhile, Earl dropped out of high school at age 15 after attending for just three months in order to take care of his mother. He would continue to look after her for the next 42 years.

"I learned the hard way, went to night school and listened, instead of talked," he said. "Anything that I have learned has come from listening and trying to develop an attentive mind."

Charlie had been a member of the North Side Vocal Club, which performed at Reverend James Poindexter's church. He may have even met his wife there. So it is likely that Earl's interest in music was attributable to his father as well. Somehow, he received formal training on the violin and his first job was at the Masonic Temple in an ensemble put together by musician and booker Thomas Howard. To make ends meet, nearly all of the musicians held down day jobs as well.

After freezing his ears during a one-year tenure with the post office, Earl secured a position at the Franklin County Court House in 1918, the first black person to do so. For the first three months, Earl recalled that nobody spoke to him except the auditor, but he was determined to hang onto the job, which he called "the best job a colored person could get." And during a period when he lost his job due to a change in administrations, he started his own insurance agency, which he later passed on to his son.

In 1918, Earl hooked up with pianist Sammy Stewart to form Sammy

Stewart's Singing Syncopators. But when the band left town for bookings, he remained behind, having decided he was committed to his job with the county auditor. Even after Stewart's band went on to make a name for itself in Detroit and, later Chicago, Earl only joined it on those occasions when he had time off. He did manage to play with band members during their fabled engagement at the Sunset Café on Chicago's Southside, filling in on bass. By then they had evolved into a symphonic jazz orchestra, similar to Paul Whiteman's orchestra. According to Earl, Louis Armstrong once sat in for their trumpeter, Eugene Hutt, but "he couldn't cut the music. He was a speller [read music slowly] and you couldn't spell there because they'd put on a class number like 'Rhapsody in Blue' or 'The William Tell Overture.'" However, Armstrong purportedly claimed he was rejected because his skin was too dark.

Having chosen to remain in Columbus, Earl formed his own ensemble. Originally called Earl Hood and his Orchestra -- or variations thereof -- he later changed the name to Earl Hood's Orchestra after he missed a gig due to illness. The ensemble almost didn't get paid when the customer learned that Earl hadn't performed with them on that occasion. From then on, Earl made it clear that they were contracting for his band and not him.

Working primarily in the Columbus-Springfield-Dayton area, Earl and his musicians averaged two engagements a week. He led one band at Indianola Park that included Percy and Eugene Lowery. Percy would later lead his own bands, earn a law degree, and become the first black member of Ohio's parole board. Over the years, Earl continued to use Sammy Stewart's arrangements, often meeting his old friend in Detroit when his band was playing there.

After the Peppe family bought Valley Dale Ballroom, Earl Hood's Orchestra was hired as the house band there for the next 30 years. "I don't want to boast," Earl said, "but because of some of the top- notch players that I had in my band, the *Pittsburgh Courier* ranked us among the top ten Negro orchestras for years." Some of his players were saxophonist Joe Thomas, who would later work with Jimmie Lunceford; trumpeter and arranger Sy Oliver, who joined Tommy Dorsey; and Harry "Sweets" Edison, who was a star with Count Basie and Frank Sinatra's favorite trumpeter.

During his tenure at Valley Dale, Earl shared the stage with Kay Kyser, Benny Goodman, Guy Lombardo, Artie Shaw with Billie Holliday,

Earl Hood and then-Valley Dale owner Lou Peppe

and many other top-rank bands. However, when World War II broke out and he lost many of his musicians to the draft, Earl consolidated his group with

Clarence Olden's Dixie Rhythm Boys, who had moved up from Kentucky. At the same time, Earl continued to work for the county and operated a large insurance agency -- General Insurance Company -- staffed with three women. However, on New Year's Eve 1951, Earl turned the band over to Olden and walked away from the music business. His asthma had gotten so bad that his doctor feared he might not live much longer. But he still had over 40 years ahead of him.

In 1980, Earl told Arnett Howard that both sides of his family had been in central Ohio for over 170 years, although he did not go into any detail. "I get a kick out of letting people who think every Black comes from Mississippi, Virginia or Georgia know that my family was here when they came," he said. "And I don't hesitate to tell them." That closely coincides with the Federal government's ban on the importation of slaves into the United States in 1808. Odds are that Earl's ancestors had been enslaved prior to settling in Ohio. In tracing his roots, it appears that both the Hoods and the Hoopers, his paternal grandfather and grandmother's families, had ties to at least two of Ohio's historic Black settlements—communities that were populated by free blacks, fugitives from slavery, and emancipated slaves prior to the Civil War.

John Henry Hood (1830-1912), Earl's grandfather, was born in Franklin, Georgia, to Charles Hood and Catharine Whitehead. Charles was from Virginia and Catharine from Georgia or New York. In 1830, there were 2,370 slaves in Franklin out of a total population of 10,107. Presumably, John Henry's parents were among the enslaved. Although it is not known how he gained his freedom, he purportedly came to Ohio as a small boy and served as a private in the 5th Regiment, U.S. Colored Heavy Artillery during the Civil War. He died of heart disease in Franklin County, Sharon Township, and is buried in Walnut Grove Cemetery.

Keziah Jane Hooper (c. 1840-unknown), Earl's grandmother, was born in Granville Township, Mercer County, Ohio, not far from the village of Carthagena. This pre-Civil War settlement was a predominantly African American community founded in 1835 by Augustus Wattles, a Quaker educator, to provide a refuge and a trade school specifically for people of color, but open t o white students as well. Prior to their arrival in Carthagena, the Hoopers had resided in a Gist Settlement in Brown County, Ohio, either Lower Camp in Scott Township or, more likely, Upper Camp in Eagle Township. There were three major Ohio Gist Settlements, all founded after the former slaves of Samuel Gist were freed in his will and brought to Ohio from Virginia.

Isaac Hooper (1806-1887), Keziah's father, was born in Richmond, Virginia. Keziah's mother, Marilda/Merilda (or Mary E.) Hart (1813-unknown), was born in Kentucky. Isaac Hooper and Marilda Hart were married in Brown County on December 24, 1834, likely having met in one of the Gist Settlements. However, in 1847-1849, Isaac paid taxes on 40 acres of land in Granville Township, Mercer County. It is not known how he obtained the money to buy the land. Unlike Mercer County, Brown County was not particularly suitable for farming. Isaac died in Columbus of consumption of the throat and is buried in Green Lawn Cemetery.

This was Earl's heritage and he was proud of it. Although he gave up the band, he was so accustomed to working that he couldn't stop completely. He still had his county job and his insurance agency. Eventually his son took over the agency, and Earl finally retired from Franklin County after 54 years of service. Five years later in 1991, he passed away at the age of 94. To the very end, he attributed his work ethic to his father Charlie's admonition to "Always give good measure and the customers will come back!" Earl is buried in Green Lawn Cemetery.

David Meyers is a lifelong resident of Columbus, Ohio. A graduate of Miami University and The Ohio State University, he has been interested in history since childhood. This has led him to write a number of non-fiction books on a variety of topics. In 2019, he was inducted into the Ohio Senior Citizens Hall of Fame in recognition of his work. Website: https://www.explodingstove.com

The city's second market house stood in State Street, west of High Street, 1818-1830.

DON'T YOU REMEMBER?

*Lida Rose McCabe recalls days when the city's market place
was in the middle of State Street, west of High Street*

Editor's note: In 1884, Columbus native Lida Rose McCabe wrote a book titled *Don't You Remember?* that recalled some of the city's early days, including this chapter on "the market place." She was only 19 at the time. We have reprinted most of that chapter, with some light editing.

Oh, well do I remember the old market place of my native town! Two years after the Capital had been laid out (1814), a crude structure that served the property holders in the vicinity for a market house, was built in the middle of High, a little south of Rich Street. But it was poorly adapted to the purpose, and three years later, the town Council declared it a nuisance, and it was accordingly abolished. Columbus was then a straggling village in a secluded forest of refuge land, so called because Congress appropriated this wild tract of country for the safety of those, who, during our revolutionary war, had fled from Canada and Nova Scotia and espoused the cause of the revolted colonies. Immediately after the old shed on High Street was torn down, the subject of locating and building a new market house was warmly agitated. Many sites were proposed, which are now comprised in the most prominent thoroughfares of the thriving Capital; as, Rich, Town, State, and Broad streets.

Property holders in the immediate neighborhood of Broadway were ceaseless in their efforts to secure the market house. They argued that Broadway, being twenty feet wider than any other street, was originally designed for that purpose in the plan of the town. Indeed, as early as 1816, Joseph Miller built a block on Broadway, known for years after as the "Buckeye House," and now as the "Hotel Gardner," opposite Capitol Square. In doing this, he was influenced by the hope, that the market house would be located nearly in front of his property. But the council decided in favor of State Street, and a larger and more convenient market house was built on that site about the year 1818. It stood in the middle of the road, some fifty yards west of High Street. The first story, the market house proper, was built of brick, while the second was made of frame and contained two well finished rooms, the property of Squire Shields, the contractor, who rented one for a printing office, keeping the other for religious purposes.

The Squire, an eccentric genius, was a well-known character in those early days. A Justice of the Peace, a Methodist Minister of the Light Order Brigade, he had many pretensions to scholarship. Besides, he was remarkably well skilled in various kinds of manual labor. A man of great evenness of character, he possessed a wonderful control over himself, and consequently was able to curb others. Gifted with an inexhaustible fund of that quick wit and rich humor proverbial of the Irish race, he was much quoted in the little town. But the versatility of the Squire's talents was perhaps nowhere so strikingly marked as in the religious dogmas he propounded to the young men, who were wont to congregate in his room over the market, attracted, we fear, more by the eccentricities of the man, than a desire for spiritual enlightenment. The Squire loved his toddy. Indeed, many unorthodox proclivities were laid at his door. On one occasion, when a bold youth asked, why he did not practice what he preached, the Squire, shaking his long finger at this skeptical sheep of his fold, said, "I teach you what is right, and I— well, I do as I please!"

After some years, he sold out his interest in the market house to John Young, who occupied the rooms for various purposes of amusement, and it was here that he introduced the first billiard table into the town. In these very rooms, too, the travelling Yankee, with that shrewd cunning with which his ancestors hoodwinked the smoke beclouded burgomasters of Amsterdam, often imposed upon the credulity of the simple town folk, with variations of Miss Jarvis's wax works, and other catch pennies of their wily ingenuity.

In 1828, the famous Kentucky orator, the silver-tongued Henry Clay, made his great speech upon the tariff, in the market place proper. In the

Henry Clay, in 1845 photo

Jackson campaign, pending at the time, the tariff was the principal question involved. Mr. Clay had come to Columbus in the interest of a law case, then being tried before the Supreme Court, and was urged to make the speech by the enthusiastic demands of the people. Long before the appointed hour, the old market place was filled with an admiring throng, gathered from far and near.

After Clay's last clarion note had died on the evening air, the scene of daily barter was magically turned into a banqueting hall. John Young, who later became proprietor of The Eagle Coffee-House," was caterer to this banquet. Henry Clay was invariably attired in some tint of green cloth, and John Young, on this memorable occasion, to emphasize his complete rejection of the Jackson party and espousal of the Clay faction, to which he had been converted by Mr. Abram McDowell, literally turned his coat by appearing in green attire. And in the stalls where the fish monger cried her wares and the gard'ner spread his vegetables, famous men of wit, power, and learning feasted, while eloquence and sparkling red wine flowed abundantly. And those who feasted, as well as those who clung to the outside of the banqueting hall, because they had come "without the wedding garment," stored in their memories the picture "bright and rare."

But at length, the old market house yielded to the changes of time. The rapid growth of the town demanded a more commodious place of trade; and when the Council, early in 1830, bought out Young's interest, the old landmark was swept away. The frame portion of it, however, still stands on the southwest corner of State and Front streets.

On the same site, the town immediately built a still larger market house - a long, one story, shed-like structure, supported on either side by six brick pillars. The eaves of the gabled roof projected far over the walls, and a wide aisle cut through the center of the building. Thus. the people were served on all sides of the stalls. On market days, which occurred three times a week, the place presented a panorama of stirring Western life. Between the rude carts of the Dutch gard'ners hobbles the square, fat form of a buxom Fraulein in a white, high starched cap, short stuff skirt, and gay 'kerchief, her rosy face now dimpling, as she pleasantly jabbers, now darkly frowning as he soundly boxes the ears of the ragged urchin that is trying to pilfer a red cheeked apple. Against a neighboring pillar thoughtfully leans a fair, flaxen haired maiden, in the folds of whose picturesque head dress, bright bodice, and flaming short skirt, still lingers the breath of the sea. With parted lips and eyelids half drawn, she dreamily looks out upon the strange bustling life, into which Fortune has suddenly thrust her. At intervals along the streets are wooden posts linked by iron chains, such as one often sees now a days in old inland towns. Hitched to these, in long lines, are horses and mules of various breeds and colors and conditions of servitude, laden with empty or inviting saddle bags, and impatiently braying or contentedly blinking in the warm sunshine.

When the roads were in a good condition, the market frequently extended along High Street, as far north as Broad and as far south as Town Street. The farmers ' great white covered wagons usually stood on the east side of the street, along the State House Square, while their stands were on the west side. Everything was for sale on the market; for fine farms were spread on either side of Alum Creek, the Scioto, Whetstone, or Olentangy. Along the Scioto for miles, corn to the height of eight or nine feet, waved their silken tassels under the fair, sunny skies. Truly, our rich valley overflowed with milk and honey.

With few, if any, bridges, the mud roads were almost impassable. Thus, there was no way of disposing of the abundant products outside of the market, except when some more sturdy or enterprising farmer would travel on foot or horseback across the mountains to sell his wares in the East. Cut off from the outside world, the home market soon became over run, and the supply being greater than the demand, the farmer was poorly paid for his labor. But later, the canal and railroads opened up facilities, and a ready market was found in the East. The farmer now began to grow rich. With

The Clinton Bank at the southwest corner of State and High streets, just to the southeast of old market place. This photo was taken in 1862. This was the first three-story building in the city and housed a store run by David W. Deshler from 1830 to 1836.

increasing wealth, he cared less to endure the hardships of his earlier days. Then it was that there sprung up, like Topsy, that respectable rogue, the huckster! In great covered wagons, he scoured the country round, buying up eggs and butter for a mere song, and selling them on the market for a whole opera.

How delightful of a summer morning to stroll through the market! The long row of stands groan under their burden of glist'ning lettuce, mellow apples, blushing beets, unsophisticated cabbages, and great yellow pumpkins, with their laughing cheeks turned to the sun. Mingled with all is the fragrance of the trailing vines, and of the wild blossoms, while above all swells the hum

- the song, the laughter and in and out weaves the thread of human life.

Ah, me, has mother earth worn out the richness of her stores, or have our eyes and palates lost their cunning, that the modern market fails to show such splendors! The burly landlord, with loud guffaw, jostles the thrifty housewife; the sly huckster's insinuating smile challenges the swarthy Yankee's glass beads and birch bark canoes, while on the outskirts of the throng loiter scores of such hang-dog men, as are often found in the vicinity of new Western settlements.

Amid the homemade blue jeans or linsey woolsey, spun and died by the wearer's wife or sweetheart, stands the stalwart form of an Englishman, still wearing the knee breeches, leggings, and silver buckles of his native land also, you may see the jolly face, great frieze coat, and black thorn stick of a son of the Emerald Isle. Now, a couple of young limbs of the law stroll through the market to sniff a breath of the morning air and coax an appetite for breakfast; stopping here, to crack a joke with a jolly farmer, there, to buy a nosegay of Nick Maury, and while waiting for the change, toss a kiss to the pretty lass in the neighboring stall.

Hark! a lull in the surging throng. Eagerly every eye turns to catch a glimpse of the morning coach, with its foaming horses dashing through the town. But come with me to the market house. In the first stall, on the north side, for many years smiled the honest face of Nick Maury, the finest gard'ner in the town, and the first florist to bring cut flowers to the market and to cultivate. I wish you could have seen him! He was a large, muscular man, a splendid specimen of the thrifty German, and with all, a stanch citizen and good neighbor. His sturdy principles won him great respectability, while his honest heart endeared him to everybody. To the market he brought the finest vegetables raised in his beautiful garden in the southern part of the city. The garden was noted for its natural spring, over whose bubbling waters drooped the languishing boughs of an old weeping willow. Here, also, he made brandy and fine wines, the secret of which he had coaxed from an old monk on the haunted Rhine.

But the market house, for the most part, was occupied by the jolly butcher boys. Ah, who does not taste yet the delicious cuts of beef with which honest old Riddle regaled the "inner man" at two and a half cents a pound? Then, there was Ed Cowling – a sturdy Johnny Bull - the cleverest of his craft; for tell me, pray, who could cut a finer mutton chop than he? Nor must we forget his neighbors, Rickly and Barnes! And while you wait your turn at the butcher's, see the crowd at the corner, watching for "Old Man Armstrong" to come along with his basket of butter. Seldom he fails, and he will not now. Bespattered with mud from head to foot, he comes galloping along; but while his short, woolen roundabout is besmeared with the slime of the river road, nary a bit has crept into the basket, which he holds aloft. From the old farmstead at Dublin, he has come, swimming the Whetstone and ploughing through the mire; for believe me, his customers would pout for a week did they fail to get a roll of "Old Armstrong's" butter. And when he lifts the snowy cloths, see, how cool and sweet and golden lies each roll! And can't you hear the piping voice of the lad, who stands on the corner of the square, crying tempting packages of perfumed lozenges?

Everywhere are chickens and turkeys, rabbits, possums, and pheasants, and great haunches of venison. And hung in long strings and buried in deep kits are Isaac Walton's adopted children - perch, bass, and suckers caught in the Scioto, whose silvery sheen is visible from the market place. But when the shadow of the Clinton Bank, which stood on the southwest corner of High and State streets, on the present site of the National Exchange, was lost in the sunshine of the full-fledged day and the market master had rung the old bell, the empty carts began to roll homeward, leaving the market place littered with the refuse of hill and valley and stream. Perhaps, a gray-haired veteran lingered to tell a crowd of urchins, some bloody tale of Indian massacre, when Franklinton, across the river, was garrisoned with British soldiers. Maybe, a farmer's wife would stop at the weaver's to see about the weaving of her week's spinning, while her liege lord dropped in at "The Tontine" to close a bargain with a horse trader.

But I have not told you that "The Tontine" was a popular coffee-house on the market square. It was a plain, two-story brick building and a favorite resort of the market people, but best known as the headquarters of the Locofocos. The appropriateness of its name, "The Tontine," no one took the trouble to question. Mr. Pike, its proprietor, was a well read, intelligent man, who, no doubt, had a purpose in calling his house after the Italian of the seventh century, who introduced the legal clause of an annuity, with the benefit of survivorship, and was complimented by having it called after him -- "Tontine."

However, the coffee-house, under this aristocratic title, failed to gain the prosperity and notoriety, which came to it later, under the more homely name of "The Tin Pan." The origin of this nick name has been variously disputed, but popular tradition tells this story: Over the coffee-house there was a large chamber, in which the Locofocos, between 1835 and '40, were wont to hold very guarded caucuses. At this time, and with this party, originated what is now so dynamite a feature of Ohio politics -- the caucus. Dram drinking, owing to the influence of the temperance societies of that day, was deemed unfashionable. Some of the scrupulous Locofocos, to avoid the censure of church going people, cleverly suggested a private "green-room." Accordingly, off the "Star Chamber" proper, a room was fitted up, in which the leaders secretly instructed and entertained the uninitiated.

On one occasion, while striving to pave the way of a prominent dignitary to a seat in the United States Senate, a number of rebellious brethren were invited into this private apartment to partake of an oyster stew. "The

Tontine," which catered to these secret conclaves, was then the only restaurant at the Capital that served oysters in chafing dishes. The exclusiveness of these secret assemblies had frequently excited jealousy; and on this occasion the mutterings became so loud, that the ring leaders were alarmed. But a storm was prevented by a happy hit of G----, of Cincinnati.

"Curse' em," said he, "the asses are jealous of our little tin pans," (referring to the vessels in which the oysters were stewed and served.) " They shall have enough to satisfy their stomachs for once."

The proprietor of "The Tontine" was ordered to prepare a large pan of mush and milk, on a certain evening, and to place it in the middle of a table in a private chamber of his coffee-house. Then with a knowing wink, the General invited all his loco friends to a tin pan supper at "The Tontine." As his guests entered on the festive night, he led them up to the tin pan and forced everyone to take a mouthful from one common spoon. This act was called Republicanism; no parade about it. All joined in the joke with hearty laughter.

The sign of lifting a spoon to the mouth became the shibboleth of the party. From this escapade sprung the phrase: "Walk up to the trough, fodder, no fodder." For ten years, thereafter, the Democratic party was known all over the State as the tin pans, and ever after the name clung to the coffee-house. "The Tin Pan" held a bewitching spell over the farmer. Scarcely had the last peal of the market bell died on the morning air than he sought its hospitable eaves, while his wife or daughters traded at the neighboring stores.

Ah, me, the changes that time brings! Who thinks today, as he strolls through James Westwater's "queenly" store and beholds himself reflected in French mirrors and Venetian glass, and confronted on every side by the potter's deftest turnings and the artist's cunning touch, that all these later day splendors tower over the ruins of a once famous wayside tavern? But it is even so.

Fifty years ago on this very spot, flourished "Russell's Tavern," a favorite hostelry of the celebrated statesmen of that day. Walk a square farther south and while you check a note at "Brook's Bank," think you, that fifty years ago on that very site, stood the popular "City Hotel?" One summer in the twenties, so the story goes, while on one of those rambles in which his heart delighted, Washington Irving found himself a quiet, unobtrusive guest, at this same hotel.

But let us get back to the market. Ah, yes, we left the women trading. Now, filling the wagons with groceries and other family needs, the farmers bid the women folks be off to their homes, while they linger round their favorite nooks. But the town seldom had charm to keep them from their country homes, save occasion of some great political excitement, such as the famous debate of '42, when the eloquent Tom Corwin and talented Thomas

Hamar crossed swords in the old market place. Twelve years had passed since Henry Clay spoke in the former market house. In the meantime, great changes had taken place in the Capital. The population had increased by four thousand souls and many towns had been laid out in the vicinity.

At the time of the debate, Corwin was candidate for re-election to the Gubernatorial chair. Ex- Governor Shannon, the defeated rival of '40, was his Democratic opponent. The campaign was drawing to a close, when the Whig State Committee challenged Governor Shannon to debate with Governor Corwin. Then in the prime of his oratorical powers, the idol of the people, Corwin was anxious to meet his opponent in debate. The challenge was accepted. But at the eleventh hour, when all the arrangements had been completed and the meeting widely advertised, the Democratic State Committee sent an apology. They said, that Governor Shannon was engaged

Tom Corwin, in an 1861 photo by Mathew Brady

to stump the northeastern part of the State and his audiences could not be disappointed. Stumping, a political feature of Kentucky, had been introduced into Ohio a few years previous to this. In the midst of the dissatisfaction, which Governor Shannon's refusal had excited, Thomas L. Hamar came to the Capital. The timely appearance of this great debater, the Whigs claimed, was a scheme devised by the Democratic State Committee. Hamar was offered as a substitute.

The scarcity of great intellect in the Democratic party of that day, had lent to Hamar's talents an uncommon lustre. A young man of brilliant prospects, he had many of Corwin's talents. What he may have lacked of the latter's brilliancy, he made up in real solidity. While political opponents in Congress, they were mutual friends and admirers in private life. Hamar was at his best in debate, while Corwin was never more powerful than in single oratory.

Corwin was anxious for the debate with Shannon, but when he heard the name of the "Black Horse," his confidence weakened. And in the warm afternoon sunshine, as they mounted the rostrum and looked over the vast sea of upturned faces, they made a striking picture. Corwin, tall, powerful, with swarthy speaking countenance; Hamar, equally commanding in form, but with the homeliest of faces. Over his low brow fell a fiery red lock, while

Alfred Kelley built this house at 282 West Broad Street, just east of where Memorial Hall is today, between 1836 and 1838. Kelley served as a state legislator for 43 years, starting in 1814. The house was torn down in 1961 to make way for the Christopher Inn.

on his head the hair stood up like quills upon the "fretful porcupine." He greatly resembled the pictures we see of General Jackson. When in repose, his homeliness was almost repulsive; but no sooner did he speak, than his face lighted up so wonderfully, that one was tempted to think him the handsomest of men.

From all parts of the State the people came. An enthusiastic throng filled the market place, clung to the trees, blockaded the steps of the Clinton Bank, and decorated the high board fence enclosing the State House and public offices. What was the subject, do you ask? That ever vexed and vexing question, the Tariff. But why speak further! Who that was present can make another hear, see, feel the siren eloquence of the debaters? It sank into the very souls of the hearers. Whether the rich tones of Corwin, as they fell in tearful pathos, or the workings of his great, dusky face, as he swayed the multitude, or the thrilling flights of eloquence and insinuating gentleness of Hamar most moved the minds or provoked the plaudits of the wild throng, who can tell?

When their voices died upon the evening air, and the deserted market house was left to feast upon the echoes, it was not settled which got the better of his opponent; nor has it been settled to this day. The Locofocos loudly claimed that Hamar was the victor, while the Whigs were equally confident that Corwin had won the day.

Alfred Kelley   *John Brough*

Fifty years have softened the prejudices of party. Today, in the laughter or admiration which these memories arouse, the politician is lost in the man. Hamar's early death in Mexico in '46, before he had an opportunity to signalize himself in battle, robbed his party and the country at large of a man of remarkable ability. But while death prevented Hamar from fulfilling the brilliant things predicted of him, it was his good fortune to give the American people the embryo of a great soldier. It was Hamar who sent Ulysses S. Grant to West Point.

And here in the old market place, in 44', Alfred Kelley debated with John Brough on the "Finances of Ohio." There were few sturdier men than Alfred Kelley. To his skill and integrity, Ohio owes that financial prosperity which has made her such a power among the States. To him, the "Father of her Internal Improvements," Ohio is indebted for the abolition of that remnant of feudal times – imprisonment for debt. To him, also, she owes the establishment of her State Banking System. A sound logician and reasoner, Kelley was utterly devoid of humor in debate. As who that recollects his tilt with Hamar can forget!

A few years more of primitive simplicity and sturdy yeoman customs, then came the giant, Progress. Mud roads, the occasion of many a long yarn and jolly story; turnpikes, with many a romance at the old toll gate, gave way to hissing steam and serpentine tracks of glistening iron. Ingenuity ran wild, and longings for wealth and Solomon's glory filled the humblest bosom. Then it was that the old market place was swept away. Ah, where are they that bartered and higgled with a smile on their lip and a laugh in their eye, a song for a penny and good will for all? In the memory, of some gray-haired pilgrim, they still live; but for the greater part:

" Their graves are scattered far and wide,
By mount and stream and sea."

Lida Rose McCabe was born in Columbus on March 3, 1865. Her parents were Irish. She graduated from Central High School in Columbus before studying at Convent Notre Dame de Sion in Paris. Besides *Don't You Remember?,* McCabe wrote several books including *Occupations and Compensations of Women, The American Girl at College* and *Ardent Adrienne: The Life of Madame de La Fayette.* She regularly contributed to numerous magazines and newspapers, including the *New-York Tribune, New York Herald, New York World,* and *Commercial Advertiser.* She died December 9, 1938, at the Madison Square Hotel in New York City.

Top of box given to a member of the OSU baseball traveling party in Korea in 1956

BUCKEYE AMBASSADORS:

The Goodwill Tour of the 1956 Ohio State Baseball Team

By JAMES TOOTLE

Local collector Tracy Martin, always on the lookout to add to his extensive assemblage of baseball-related materials, was browsing in an antique shop in the Short North area of Columbus. After asking the proprietor if he had any baseball items and being informed that the shop did not handle sports memorabilia, he was about to leave when the owner remembered he had one item in his back room that might be of some interest.

The shop owner stepped away for a few minutes and returned with an elegant black lacquer box. The contents included a neatly arranged pack of Picayune brand cigarettes, a supply of wooden matches, and a metal ash tray. An inscription inside the lid provided the reason the antique dealer thought a baseball collector might be interested in the box:

TO: OHIO STATE BASEBALL TEAM
KOREA NATIONAL BASEBALL ASSN
JULY 29, 1956

Curious about the baseball-related inscription, Martin purchased the box. Since the early 1990s, Tracy Martin and I have been members of the

Ohio History Connection's 1860-era Ohio Village Muffins vintage base ball (two words in the nineteenth century) program. This shared interest in the history of the national pastime has led to many conversations over the years about baseball cards, uniforms, balls, bats, photographs, board games, catcher's equipment, and other collectibles. Shortly after his acquisition, he showed me the box and asked if I knew anything about the inscription. I did not, but agreed to look into the matter and share any findings.

Several possible explanations came to mind. Did the Korean team come to the United States in 1956 and play in Columbus? Did the OSU and Korean teams meet in a tournament somewhere? Did the Buckeye team travel to Korea?

Research in the *Columbus Dispatch; The Lantern* (OSU student newspaper); the *Makio* (OSU yearbook), and materials in the University Archives, revealed the compelling, but largely forgotten, story of an extensive "Goodwill Tour" to the Far East by the Ohio State baseball team in the summer of 1956.

The coach of the Ohio State baseball team was Marty Karow, who had won seven varsity letters at OSU in football, basketball, and baseball in the mid-1920s. He had been named an All-American in football in 1926 and served as team captain. After a brief major league career (six games and 11 plate appearances as an infielder with the 1927 Boston Red Sox) and four seasons in the minors (1927-1930), Karow went into coaching. Following coaching positions at Texas, the Naval Academy, and Texas A&M, Karow returned to his alma mater as head baseball coach in 1950.

The varsity baseball roster for 1956 included three exceptionally talented two-sport athletes who were more well known during their college years for their success in their "other" sport. Senior center fielder Howard "Hopalong" Cassady, of Columbus Central High School, had led the OSU football team to a Big Ten and national championship in 1954, when the Buckeyes defeated USC in the January 1, 1955 Rose Bowl. In 1955, OSU won another Big Ten championship as Cassady was named the winner of the prestigious Heisman Trophy as the best player in college football.

Sophomore pitcher Galen Cisco played fullback on the football team. Cisco was co-captain of the 1957 Big Ten and national championship team that defeated Oregon in the January 1, 1958 Rose Bowl.

Sophomore left fielder Frank Howard of Columbus South High School, earned All-American honors in basketball in 1957. He was also named as an All-American in baseball, but was far better known as the basketball Buckeyes' leading scorer and rebounder.

The April 2, 1956 edition of *The Lantern* listed the starting infield as Don Kelley at first, Dick Burkley at second, Ron Shay at shortstop, and captain Chuck Ellis at third. Jack Purvis was the regular catcher. *The*

Hop Cassady is better known as a football player, but also starred in baseball at OSU.

Lantern said the outfielders had "exactly what it takes to qualify for the job: speed, a good arm and all three hit the long ball:" Bob Schnabel was in left, Cassady in center, and Howard, who "hits the ball with as much authority as anyone on the team," in right. The pitching staff had been thinned by graduation with only Bill Soter and Skip Burns (who had a sore arm) returning. The article said Karow would have to "experiment further with the rookie chuckers" to find other starting pitchers. Although it was not known at the time, Cisco would emerge from this category as an outstanding starter.

A review of newspaper stories published in March and early April 1956 reported on typical pre-season topics related to the prospects for the OSU team repeating as Big Ten champions, including the possible impact of

Frank Howard hit 382 home runs in 16 major league seasons.

three basketball players -- Bob Schnabel, Norm Steagall, and Howard -- who would be joining the team late. The continuing search for dependable starting pitching was a recurring theme. One *Lantern* article recapped the team's spring trip to Florida on which they compiled a 6-3 record. Mention was made of Steagall working as a back-up catcher and infielder Vern Barkstall of Columbus North High School earning more playing time. Another article mentioned the season opener at Ohio University which, as often happens to early spring games, was rained out.

Nothing in the papers indicated anything special was in store for the

1956 team until the April 10 issue of *The Lantern* carried the headline: "Buckeye Baseballers to Tour Japan" and announced "the Ohio State University baseball team will make an exhibition tour of Japan this summer." The opposition would be "Japanese University teams and Armed Services teams at U.S. bases."

"Official confirmation from the Department of the Army concerning transportation reached the athletic department yesterday where it was released by Wilbur Snypp, director of athletic publicity." While the invitation had come from the Department of the Army, the trip would be "sponsored by all the services, with all expenses being paid by the U.S. Services Public Relations Fund."

Additional perspective on international travel included the observation that "This will be the most extensive trip that any Ohio State team has ever taken. Japanese teams played here in the 1920s but this will be the first Buckeye trip there." The article mentioned that the University of Southern California team made of a similar trip the previous summer "with a great deal of success." The article concluded that the trip "was approved by Western Conference (Big Ten) officials."

The regular season schedule continued with a games against Western Michigan, Miami and Xavier. Rainy and threatening weather conditions caused a series of delays and postponements of these contests. The games that were played occurred in cold, damp weather. *Lantern* columnist John Phillips wrote of his concern that all these weather interruptions were causing the Buckeyes to play too few games before meeting their Big Ten opponents.

The Buckeyes opened the Big Ten season against Michigan State, which finished second to OSU in 1955, followed by a doubleheader in Ann Arbor with Michigan. MSU was defeated 8-7 on "a 400 plus ft. homer over the centerfield wall" by Frank Howard that put Ohio State in the lead to stay. The Michigan games were postponed due to rain. The "Sportsgab" column in *The Lantern* which carried the byline of Bill Soter, starting pitcher and journalism student, listed the likely contenders to dethrone the defending-champion Buckeyes.

An article in the April 27 Lantern provided more information on the trip to Japan. The departure date was reported as June 15, with a stop in Honolulu before the team continued on to Japan. "After Japan, the Bucks will move on to Okinawa for a week and then play for a week in Korea." This mention of Korea establishes the likely occasion for the presentation of the black lacquer box to the visiting OSU team.

A May 3 column in the Lantern reported that "Baseball coach Marty Karow is angered by his team's 'complacency.' He says they're more concerned with the forthcoming Japan trip than they are with winning ball games." He may have had a point, given the excitement over the trip apparent in the tone of the April 27 column and subsequent articles on the trip.

OSU baseball team preparing to take off on its Goodwill Tour. Sophomore Vern Barkstall (far right) became OSU's first Black baseball captain as a senior in 1958.

A May 29 column by pitcher-sportswriter Soter provided an update on the team's itinerary. The latest plan called for the Bucks to leave Columbus June 15 for San Francisco to begin a schedule of 35 games with "Army, Navy, Air Force and Japanese teams" and tour "Japan, Korea, Hawaii, Okinawa and possibly Guam." From Travis Air Force Base, the team was scheduled to fly to Honolulu, then to Japan for their first game with the Camp Zama service team in Tokyo. According to Soter, "the Bucks are to conclude their once-in-a-lifetime trip in Hawaii with a tentative contest with the University of Hawaii. The Karowmen will also visit Kauai, an island off the coast of Hawaii...the home of Scarlet outfielder Warren Mitzutani. A game has been scheduled there so that Mizutani's countrymen can see him in action."

The rest of the regular season went reasonably well, with Ohio State posting an overall winning record of 18-7-1 and a Big Ten record of 9-3. However, Minnesota won the 1956 conference championship with a record of 11-2 and an overall record of 33-9. The Buckeyes finished second, followed by Wisconsin (8-4) and Michigan (6-5).

Next was the much-anticipated trip to Japan. Records indicate that the Ohio State travelling party was limited to 24 individuals -- 21 players, an equipment manager, a trainer, and Coach Karow. But photos and articles clearly show Athletic Director Richard Larkins also made the trip. The tour would last approximately two months with the team returning sometime in the first or second week of August.

'As described by *Columbus Dispatch* writer Bill Breslin, "The trip to

Japan was made in a series of hops, long and short, that included stops at San Francisco, Hickam Field in Hawaii, Wake Island, and finally the Dai Iti Hotel in Tokyo where they stayed for a month." Breslin reported that according to a diary kept by pitcher Bill Meade, "the days between games were filled with a steady diet of tours and side trips to the streets of Tokyo and surrounding towns."

The tour got off to a great start as Galen Cisco pitched an 8-0 shutout win over the Army team from Camp Zama. A *Dispatch* article of June 21, reported that "Ohio State's baseball team played to a crowd of 55,000 in Tokyo Wednesday (June 20) in the first game of its exhibition tour of Japan, according to word received by the Athletic Department." Cassady and Howard each had three hits against the Camp Zama starting pitcher, Don Nuxhall, brother of Cincinnati pitcher Joe Nuxhall. A game against Rikkyo University had to be rescheduled due to rain, but the Buckeyes won their next contest 12-3 over Johnson AFB.

Leading off its coverage of the next two games, the *Dispatch* informed its readers that "Bill Soter, erstwhile starting pitcher, has been putting his sturdy right arm to work with the pen, as well, and we are indebted to him for these reports from Tokyo." Two Japanese university teams provided much tougher opposition than the American service teams. In a doubleheader that was nationally televised and played before a crowd of 15,000 in Meiji Stadium, the Buckeyes lost to Rikkyo University 5-2, then played to a 3-3 tie with Waseda University in a game that was called after nine innings

In the July 5 edition of the *Dispatch*, columnist Paul Hornung drew on Bill Soter's reports from Japan to write of Frank Howard being "a slugging sensation in the Far East." A long homer led OSU to a 6-5 win over Nihon University and paced by "another smoking shot over the 340-foot mark." OSU "whitewashed Chou U., 4-0," behind the pitching of Soter. The wins brought OSU's record to 4-1-1.

Hornung also wrote glowingly about the way the OSU players were conducting themselves. "On the good will side, the Buckeyes seem to be accomplishing their purpose, too. The Japanese press commended Karow's men...for their 'strong competitive spirit and admirable sportsmanship.'" Hornung observed that "it comes as no surprise, of course, that the Buckeyes are representing their university and their nation so nobly."

The July 9 edition of the *Dispatch* reported how Howard was "still laying down a barrage of cannon blasts in the Far East," hitting two long homers in a 9-2 win over Mishawaka AFB on June 29 and "four vicious singles in a 13-0 romp over Tachikawa AFB" on July 3. On the next day, it was only 55 degrees, but slugger Howard was described as being as "hot as any firecracker on this July 4th in Japan," as he hit his sixth homer in nine games and increased his RBI total to 24 as the Buckeyes "waltzed to a 19-0"

Galen Cisco spent nine years in the major leagues as a player and 26 as a coach.

victory behind the no-hit pitching of Soter.

A pattern was becoming established as the Goodwill Tour continued -- wins by wide margins over the service teams but close scores (including some losses) in games with the Japanese university teams. After reporting that the Buckeyes were "enjoying a great experience on the team's Goodwill Tour," Hop Cassady confirmed "some of the service teams aren't too formidable opponents" and that "the Japanese college teams are a lot better." He marveled that the Japanese pitchers "really have control. I think they could go all day without walking anybody," adding "Baseball is their big sport over there."

Cassady was also effusive in his praise of the power hitting of teammate Frank Howard, referred to by Paul Hornung as "the muscle man from South High." "Man, he's murdering the ball," Cassady said. "He hits one out of the park about every game. One game he hit one over the centerfield fence, which was about 350 feet, and I swear it went almost as far out of the park as in. He's as good as some guys in the major leagues right now!"

Cassady had to leave the baseball team in mid-July, as had been expected since the trip began. Accompanied by Athletic Director Larkins, he flew home to play in the College All-Star Game, an annual pre-season football game held from 1934 to 1976 in Chicago. The popular game pitted the defending NFL champion against a team of college seniors from the previous year. As the 1955 Heisman Trophy winner, Cassady was expected to be an important contributor to the college team. Interviewed upon his return, Cassady said "It was a great trip and we had a real good time." Asked about the quality of the Japanese college teams being higher than expected, he was consistent in his praise of the pitchers. "They've got real good control. They hardly ever walk anybody but they aren't too fast. The big difference between them and the Big Ten pitchers is their control."

Coach Karow, when interviewed by the Dispatch's Breslin about the ability of the Japanese college teams, also remarked, "They had terrific control. They weren't afraid to come in with that curve when they were in a hole, and they get it across, too. Almost all the Buckeyes agreed as to the quality of their Japanese opponents. They played good, tight baseball, preferring to play for one run and then hoping their pitcher could stop the Bucks."

Cassady was also complimentary regarding the Japanese fans. "Over there they all play ball. They love it. They play ball where they work and even have a catch during their lunch hours."

After Cassady returned home, he signed his first professional football contract for $15,000 with the Detroit Lions. At what was described in the *Dispatch* as a "festive luncheon at the Deshler-Hilton Hotel," the newspaper called him "the highest paid rookie in professional sports" and noted that "the contract was flown down to Columbus by the Detroit officials who felt that snaring a prize like the Columbus red-head merited more than a casual signing."

After Cassady's departure from the baseball team, Warren Mitzutani took over in centerfield for the Buckeyes. OSU easily defeated three Air Force base teams, but "Aichi University kept up the pressure that the Japanese universities have been putting on the Bucks." Trailing 1-0 in the eighth, OSU scored a run on clutch singles by Steagall and Burkley to salvage a 1-1 tie. On July 27, the *Dispatch* reported "two very lopsided wins, 20-0 over Camp Kure All-Stars and 19-0 over Ashiya.

After the Camp Kure game, Breslin wrote that the OSU team visited Hiroshima and "viewed the historic crater" made by the first atomic bomb in 1945. Throughout the tour, visits to sites of historical and cultural importance, as well as daily interaction with their hosts, provided the team members with educational experiences that went far beyond the scores of the baseball games.

Breslin reported that the next two games were "a 2-1 loss to Kwansai U., and a 1-1 tie with Rituemi U." After the Rituemi game, "the entire squad was taken to the world famous Takarazuka Theater to see the Takarazuka Revue.

The OSU team then flew to Korea, where Breslin wrote that "they proceeded to clobber their first hosts, Osan AFB, 12-1. But near Seoul they ran afoul of Camp 24 and were outslugged 10-5," a rare loss to a service team. The next two games were wins on July 29 over the baseball team of the ROK (Republic of Korea) Army, a member of the Korea National Baseball Association. Since the date of the games matches the inscription on the lid of the black lacquer box, it was these games with the ROK Army team that provided the occasion for the presentation of the box to the visiting OSU team.

Next was a trip to Okinawa, where OSU lost to the Army All-Stars 4-0. Breslin reported that after viewing a film on the Battle of Okinawa, the Buckeyes bounced back with a 7-1 win over the Air Force All-Stars and a 16-1 win over the Marine All-Stars. From Okinawa, the team flew "back to the Osaka Hotel in Tokyo and a round of parties and dinners for the soon-to-depart Buckeyes.

On August 10, the team left Japan for the Hawaiian Islands. They stayed at Hickam Field and enjoyed a day of swimming at Waikiki Beach. The stop included a game with the Navy Base team, which OSU lost 6-1. Breslin describes how the Buckeyes then "bounced back" from their recent loss "to thrill Warren Mitzutani's hometown crowd at Lihue on the Island if Kauai. Batting in the second spot, Miz belted the first pitch for a home run. The little outfielder's swat could not have come at a more opportune time since he was being honored that day by his hometown fans. Riding the crest of Miz's homer, the Bucks went on to edge Kawai, 4-3." The final game of the tour was played the next day with the University of Hawaii and was won by OSU, 4-3. From there, the Buckeyes flew home.

OSU coach Marty Karow

The final record for the Goodwill Tour of 1956 was 21-6-3, but, as Bill Breslin of the *Dispatch* pointed out, the trip was about much more than wins and losses. "It's the almost unanimous opinion of Coach Marty Karow and the ball players that the trip provided them with a unique educational experience."

A decade after the tour, Coach Marty Karow led OSU to three straight College World Series appearances, 1965-67, winning the national championship in 1966. He was named to the Baseball Coaches Hall of Fame in 1973 and retired in 1975. Hop Cassady played eight years in the NFL and was a member of the NFL champion Detroit Lions in 1957. After football, he worked in the New York Yankees organization and was a coach for many years for the Columbus Clippers. Galen Cisco pitched for three MLB teams (1961-69), then had a 28-year career as a pitching coach for five teams including the 1992 and 1993 World Series champion Toronto Blue Jays. Frank Howard was rookie of the year with the Los Angeles Dodgers in 1980 and a member of the 1963 World Series champions. Traded to Washington, he was a four-time All-Star and two-time home run champion with the Senators. All four are members of the OSU Athletics Hall of Fame.

Now that the story of the black lacquer box is known, is the wish of collector Tracy Martin, who rescued it from the back room of an antique shop, that it should go back to where he feels it belongs. Arrangements are being made for him to donate it to the Ohio State baseball team's display area, so that current and future OSU players and coaches will be aware of this historic chapter from the program's past.

James Tootle, PhD, is a member of the Board of Trustees of the Columbus History Society and is chair of the Publications Committee. He retired as the assistant dean of The Ohio State University College of Arts and Sciences. He is a member of the Society for American Baseball Research and is the author of *Baseball in Columbus*. He can be reached at jtootle@columbus.rr.com.

This is how the black lacquer box looks when opened, with cigarettes, ash tray, matches and inscription.

BOOK REVIEW

OHIO BUCKEYE CANDY, A SWEET HISTORY

By AMY HUNTER

If you live in Ohio, especially Columbus, you've had a buckeye candy. For those who don't know (and I pity you!) buckeyes are a chocolate and peanut butter confection that looks like the nut from a buckeye tree. With a sweet peanut butter fudge-like filling shaped into a ball and dipped in chocolate, they're wildly simple to make, and you'll almost always find some on an Ohio Christmas cookie platter.

I thought I knew everything about these confections — after all, you don't need much skill to make them, and the flavor combo is a well-known hit everywhere. You may think the same until you read *Ohio Buckeye Candy: A Sweet History* by Renee Casteel Cook.

At first glance, you may be wondering what exactly this book contains. The cover shows clear, beautiful photos of buckeye candies

Ohio Buckeye Candy, A Sweet History
By Renee Casteel Cook
The History Press
160 Pages
Release Date: August 7, 2023

in all their chocolate and peanut butter glory, while the middle of the book has beautiful photos of buckeyes drizzled with white chocolate, perched atop cupcakes with mountains of peanut butter frosting, and tucked into pies and sundaes with plenty of chocolate and peanut butter expertly drizzled on top.

You're forgiven if you think it's full of recipes (although there is a single recipe for The Original Buckeye Candy in the Introduction.) Instead, you get a lot of history, along with all the major players in the buckeye candy game, plus all the latest candy shops trying to give their customers their own re-creations of the classic version.

As a self-professed chocoholic, I will admit that I have been to a good number of the candy shops in this book, and probably had buckeyes from quite a few. But I've never thought about the history, because who thinks of candy as anything but something to indulge your sweet tooth. I've walked past the giant buckeye at Anthony Thomas without thinking about who made it and how, and when I go to the Goodie Shop in my neighborhood, there are always a few buckeyes tucked in my bag. If you're an Ohio native, buckeyes are a just another part of your way of life, another part of the camaraderie of living in Ohio, whether you spend your fall Saturday's cheering on the Buckeye football team, or eating buckeye candies by the dozen.

I have just never questioned the history of these places as I've eaten these tasty treats. Who came up with the idea for these delectable creations? If you've ever asked yourself this question, this is the book for you.

The introduction gives you all of the history of these sweet treats and even how the term "buckeye" came to be. Perhaps one of the most interesting stories in the book is that of Gail Lucas, a student at The Ohio State University who received some chocolate peanut butter balls from her mother at Christmas. Recreating them, she remarked to her husband that they looked like the school's namesake tree nut. Calling them buckeyes, she made them for friends and family for years, sharing the recipe with only one friend, who years later submitted the buckeye recipe to the OSU alumni magazine in 1973 in her own name. It wasn't until a decade later in 1983 that Gail decided to set the record straight and publish the recipe using her maiden name, Tabor, in the Arizona Republic. It's unclear whether Gail made any money from buckeye candies, but it does make clear that if you think you have a winning recipe, don't share it with anyone.

Once you've gotten the history down, it's time to get to the essence of the book — the chocolate shops. When I first picked up the book, even before reading the introduction, I skimmed through the list of shops and immediately fanned the pages until I got to the ones I know and love. I think that's everyone's first reaction to a book like this; if your favorite place is in there, that's the page you're going to first.

With twenty-one shops in the book, the author made sure you'll find a little bit of everything, from classic candy shops to quaint neighborhood bakeries, and even a bakery that makes buckeyes for dogs. Several of the shops have the word "buckeye" in the name, indicating that that's all they sell. For some, this is true. The Buckeye Lady, a small shop on High St. in Columbus, sells buckeyes exclusively. But if you go, plan for enough time to choose your flavor, because in addition to traditional chocolate and peanut butter, they have dozens of flavors including mainstays like cinnamon roll cheesecake (what!) This is in addition to seasonal flavors like candy corn in the fall and eggnog in the winter.

But what if you want something with the spirit of a traditional buckeye, but not necessarily a bite-sized chocolate peanut butter treat? The Buckeye co. in Findlay, Ohio has buckeye dip, buckeye cookies, and a variety of buckeye "bombs" which are a quarter pound of buckeyes in flavors like DINO BOMB or Unicorn Dreams. Haute Chocolate in Cincinnati has buckeye brownies, and The Chocolate Cafe in Columbus has cakes, cupcakes, milkshakes, and martinis, all buckeye flavored. It is undeniably a great time to be alive if you're a fan of chocolate and peanut butter!

What if you're looking for something fancy? While homemade buckeyes hold a certain kind of rustic charm, sometimes you want something that will impress. If that's the case, you're in luck because Lohcally Artisan Chocolates on the picturesque streets of Powell, a Columbus suburb, has the most elegant buckeyes you've ever seen. Perfectly smooth in shape with glossy, colorful decorative touches, these will certainly be the hit you're looking for.

The author definitely gets to the heart and soul of these shops, as each section tells you everything you wanted to know about these businesses. I imagine her visiting the shops and talking about chocolate and peanut butter until she herself was sick of it (as if). You'll learn about how Anthony Zanetos immigrated from Greece and started the one-and-only Anthony Thomas and how his great-great grandson still runs the operations with the same dedication and tenacity as Zanetos did, bigger and more widely known than his great-great grandfather ever could have imagined more than a century later.

Or how Marsha Smith began making buckeyes in her home kitchen, like all of us do around the holidays. She started selling her homemade candies at neighborhood garage sales in 1984 and now sells her creations in grocery stores around the country. Perhaps her most proud achievement is selling them to The Ohio State University, where they are available in both Ohio Stadium and the Schottenstein Center to sports fans around the state, eager to indulge in the classic candy while proudly cheering on their favorite teams all year long.

As I was reading this book, I imagined the author asking questions, snapping photos, and visiting chocolate shops for a purpose other than lazily choosing which treat I'll be indulging in this time. It is certainly a labor of love, and it shows.

Whatever you're aiming to find in the pages of this extensively researched book, I think you'll find it here. Whether you want to try a new chocolate experience, or are thinking of starting a buckeye business yourself and need a little inspiration, it's all here. I was delighted to find that the author has two other books, *The Columbus Food Truck Cookbook*, and *Ohio Ice Cream: A Scoop of Columbus History,* both of which I can't wait to get my hands on.

Now, if you'll excuse me, I have a few chocolate shops I've got to check out.

Amy Hunter is a culinary school graduate, food writer and photographer. You can find out about her work or contact her at tinyredkitchen.com.

PHOTO AND MAP CREDITS

5 – Columbus Metropolitan Library
6 – Columbus Metropolitan Library
7 – Columbus Metropolitan Library
8 – Columbus Metropolitan Library
9 – Columbus Metropolitan Library
11 – Columbus Metropolitan Library
12 – Columbus Metropolitan Library
14 – Columbus Metropolitan Library
16 – Columbus Metropolitan Library
18 – Columbus Metropolitan Library
21 – Unknown artist, from an 1817 print.
22 – *History of the City of Columbus, Capital of Ohio*, 1892.
24 – National Archives
26 – Metropolitan Museum of Art, Southworth and Hawes photo.
28 – Columbus Metropolitan Library
29 – Bob Hunter photo
30 – Flickr
33 – Bob Hunter photo
35 – *Ohio Sentinel*
37 – AIM Music
38 – Columbia Records
39 – Amy Records
40 – MCA Records
41 – Doug Tracy collection
44 – *Columbus Dispatch*
46 – Listen for the Jazz Archives
47 – *Columbus Dispatch*
48 – Bob Thomas
50 – Columbus Metropolitan Library
52 – Library of Congress
54 – Columbus Metropolitan Library
58 – Library of Congress
59 = Library of Congress
60 – Columbus Metropolitan Library
60 – *Harper's Daily*
62 – James Tootle
64 – Ohio State University Archives
65 – Ohio State University Archives
67 – Ohio State University Archives
69 – Ohio State University Archives
71– Ohio High School Baseball Coaches Association
72 -- James Tootle

Cover photo -- Columbus Metropolitan Library

MAKE A CONTRIBUTION
TO OUR CAPITAL CAMPAIGN

The Columbus Historical Society recently purchased Engine House #6, 540 West Broad Street, from the Metropolitan Housing Authority, and is in the process of restoring the building for use as the society's permanent home. When it is finished, it will include a museum, research library, and community events space, as well as home for our growing historical archives. The prominent architectural firm of Schooley Caldwell is doing the design work.

The project has received broad support from the city, county and state government officials; community leaders, businesses, and other not-for-profit organizations. Support has come from the Columbus City Council, the Columbus mayor's office, the Mid-Ohio Regional Planning Commission, Columbus Foundation, Columbus Landmarks Foundation, Franklinton Board of Trade and state legislators. Our state capital funding request was supported by the Columbus Partnership.

But to date, we still have raised half of the estimated cost of over $3 million for the project and are greatly in need of more financial support. Won't you please consider a contribution to both the project and the preservation of history in our community?

All donors to our general funds at the $100 level or above will automatically receive dual deluxe level membership.

Donor categories:

- Friend: Up to $99
- Contributor: $100 to $499
- Supporter: $500 to $999
- Partner: $1000 to $4,999
- Leadership Circle: $5,000 and above.

Artist's rendering of Engine House #6 after Columbus Historical Society renovation

Engine House #6 was built in 1890 and was in service from 1890 until 1966. It was the home of the Columbus Fire Department's first emergency squad in 1934. After its service as a Franklinton fire station ended, it later became home of Jimmy Rea Electronics.

Look for a story on the history of Engine House #6 in an upcoming issue of *Columbus History, A Journal of the Columbus Historical Society*.

Monday, April 27, 1931. . . Ad in the *Columbus Dispatch*